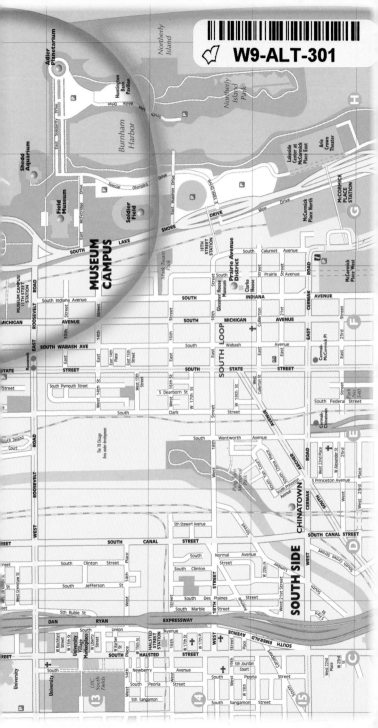

Fodor's
25 Best

CHICAGO

How to Use This Book

KEY TO SYMBOLS	
✚ Map reference to the accompanying fold-out map	🛳 Nearest riverboat or ferry stop
✉ Address	♿ Facilities for visitors with disabilities
☎ Telephone number	❓ Other practical information
🕓 Opening/closing times	▷ Further information
🍴 Restaurant or café	ℹ Tourist information
🚊 Nearest rail station	✋ Admission charges: Expensive (over $20), Moderate ($13–$20) and Inexpensive ($13 or less)
🚇 Nearest subway (Metro) station	
🚌 Nearest bus route	

This guide is divided into four sections

● Essential Chicago: An introduction to the city and tips on making the most of your stay.
● Chicago by Area: We've broken the city into five areas, and recommended the best sights, shops, entertainment venues, nightlife and places to eat in each one. Suggested walks help you to explore on foot.
● Where to Stay: The best hotels, whether you're looking for luxury, budget or something in between.
● Need to Know: The info you need to make your trip run smoothly, including getting about by public transportation, weather tips, emergency phone numbers and useful websites.

Navigation In the Chicago by Area chapter, we've given each area its own color, which is also used on the locator maps throughout the book and the map on the inside front cover.

Maps The fold-out map with this book is a comprehensive street plan of Chicago. The grid on this fold-out map is the same as the grid on the locator maps within the book. We've given grid references within the book for each sight and listing.

Contents

Introducing Chicago

Poet Carl Sandburg called Chicago "City of the big shoulders." Former Mayor Richard J. Daley boasted it's "the city that works." It's nicknamed "The Windy City," not because of its weather, but because of its long-winded politicians. Pick your interpretation—city of brawn and industry, brash and bustling, modern and innovative—it's all here in Chicago.

In the 1800s, as the city grew, a distinct breed of entrepreneurs and hucksters made their way to the city's Lake Michigan shores seeking opportunity. No amount of tragedy could persuade them from their enterprises, be they legal or not. Two days after the Great Chicago Fire of 1871 had reduced most of the city to ashes, one real-estate broker posted a sign reading: "All gone but wife, children and energy."

Afterward, the city shucked its 19th-century past and became the most modern metropolis in the country, if not the world, home to the first skyscraper and a new Prairie School of architecture in sync with the low, limitless horizon of the region. Musicians came and amped up the blues. Gangsters grabbed a piece of the action and held on. Immigrants flocked here from every corner of the world, bringing their culture and foods to Chicago's neighborhoods. Everyone thought big. "Make no little plans," said former Chicago city planner and architect Daniel Burnham, "they have no magic to stir men's blood."

The spirit of optimism that marks the commercial aspects of the city is distinct on a personal level, too. It's a common stereotype that Midwesterners are friendly; Chicagoans are often that and more—honest, opinionated and nice. It takes optimism to emigrate and Chicago received wave after wave of Scandinavians and Germans early on, later welcoming large communities of Irish, Polish and Mexicans. Chicago is perhaps the most American city of all.

FACTS AND FIGURES

- Residents: 2.72 million
- Languages spoken: 150
- Museums: 80
- Parks: 601
- Third largest city in the US
- Lakefront bike paths: 18 miles (29km)
- The "Historic Route 66" begins in downtown Chicago on Adams Street, in front of the Art Institute of Chicago.

MUSICAL CHICAGO

Jazz has thrived in the city since the 1920s when New Orleans' innovators moved north. Louis Armstrong struck out on his own with the "Hot Five" recordings he made in town. Later, African Americans moving up from the rural South settled in and took the traditional blues music electric. Both jazz and blues clubs still entertain today.

EDIBLE CHICAGO

In the early 20th century, Chicago was a meat-and-potatoes place, home of stockyards and slaughterhouses and the railroad hub transporting beef to the outer regions. Steak houses, deep-dish pizza and hot dogs continue the tradition of substantive eating in Chicago. But in the past 25 years, the city has nurtured a modern band of chefs to become one of the most innovative places to eat in the US.

DESIGN CHICAGO

Architects and entrepreneurs engineered Chicago's phoenix after the Great Fire, inventing the skyscraper in the rebuilding. Daniel Burnham had bold plans for Chicago's front yard of parks that buffer city and shore. Frank Lloyd Wright founded his Prairie School of design here. Later, innovators such as Mies van der Rohe also left their mark and bolstered Chicago's reputation as a great architectural city.

A Short Stay in Chicago

DAY 1

Morning Start your stay with a 9am stroll around **Millennium Park** (▷ 50), then walk across Frank Gehry's bridge to see and photograph the reflections on the highly polished bean-shape sculpture by Anish Kapoor.

Mid-morning Walk the two blocks over to the **Art Institute of Chicago** (▷ 44). Doors open at 10.30 each day, and lines form at least 15 minutes prior. It's worth the effort to have the Impressionist galleries briefly to yourself.

Lunch Take a break and soak up the Loop atmosphere at **Atwood** (▷ 37), just a few blocks northwest of the museum on Washington and State streets.

Afternoon Head to Randolph and Wabash, where you can catch the elevated train, aka the **El** (▷ 26). Take the Brown Line bound for Kimball. Get off at the Belmont stop and walk to the opposite platform to catch the train heading back to the Loop.

Mid-afternoon Take a leisurely walk around the Loop to admire the **public sculptures** installed there (▷ 25). Start your walk with the unnamed Picasso in Daley Center Plaza, then continue on to the Calder at the Federal Center Plaza and, finally, see the Jean Dubuffet sculpture at the James R. Thompson Center.

Dinner Head for **Gino's East** (▷ panel, 80) for an authentic taste of Chicago's deep-dish pizza.

Evening Get tickets to **Second City** (▷ 67) for a good guffaw over Chicago-style humor, which is topical and partly improvised.

DAY 2

Morning Hop on the 10am **Chicago Architecture Foundation Center River Cruise** (▷ 24) offered by the Chicago Architecture Center. The tours are a big draw so reserve before coming to town.

Mid-morning Disembark the boat and walk up the **Magnificent Mile** (▷ 68), the stretch of Michigan Avenue that runs from the Chicago River up to Oak Street, to check out the upscale shopping district and a number of architectural landmarks including, the **Wrigley Building** (▷ 72), **Tribune Tower** (▷ 72) and **875 N. Michigan Avenue**, formerly called the John Hancock Center (▷ 58–59).

Lunch Pass the fine jewelry kiosks and enjoy Middle Eastern fare at **Oasis Café** (▷ 38), serving falafel and kebob sandwiches.

Afternoon Rent bikes at **Navy Pier** (▷ 64) and take a spin on the Lake Michigan shoreline past the popular **Oak Street** (▷ 71) and **North Avenue** (▷ 66) beaches to appreciate how Chicagoans play.

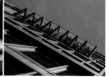

Mid-afternoon Ascend 875 N. Michigan Avenue to **360 CHICAGO** (▷ 58–59) to see the city from 1,000ft (305m) above the ground. If you dare, try TILT, the thrill experience where you stand in a glass box and tilt over the edge of the skyscraper.

Dinner Sit down to order a glass of wine or cocktail perfectly paired to seafood as well as small, shareable plates at the Bib Gourmand-winning seafood restaurant **GT Fish & Oyster** (▷ 79).

Evening Take a cab to **Buddy Guy's Legends** (▷ 35) on the near South Side to catch a few sets of the blues before calling it a night.

ESSENTIAL CHICAGO TOP 25

These pages are a quick guide to the Top 25, which are described in more detail later. Here they are listed alphabetically and the tinted background shows the area they are in.

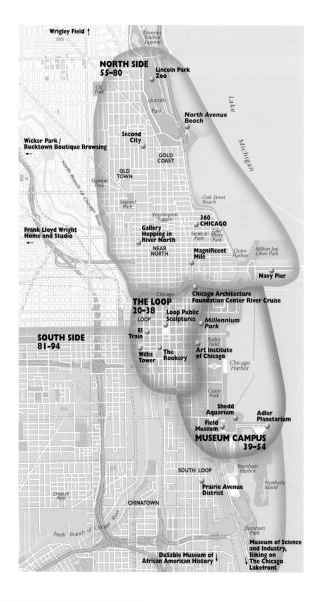

Wrigley Field ↑

NORTH SIDE
55-80

Lincoln Park Zoo

Diversey Harbor Lagoon

Oz Park

Lincoln Park

North Avenue Beach

Lake Michigan

Wicker Park / Bucktown Boutique Browsing ←

Second City

North Branch of Chicago River

GOLD COAST

OLD TOWN

Stanton Park

Seward Park

Oak Street Beach

Frank Lloyd Wright Home and Studio ←

Washington Square

Gallery Hopping in River North

360 CHICAGO

Seneca Park *Lake Shore Park*

NEAR NORTH

Magnificent Mile

Outer Harbor

Milton Lee Olive Park

Navy Pier

Chicago

Chicago Architecture Foundation Center River Cruise

THE LOOP
20-38

LOOP

Loop Public Sculptures

Millennium Park

Butler Field

SOUTH SIDE
81-94

El Train

Willis Tower

The Rookery

Art Institute of Chicago

Chicago Harbor

Grant Park

Shedd Aquarium

Adler Planetarium

Field Museum

MUSEUM CAMPUS
39-54

Burnham Harbor

Northerly Island

SOUTH LOOP

Prairie Avenue District

Dyon Park

CHINATOWN

South Branch of Chicago River

Burnham Park

Museum of Science and Industry, Biking on The Chicago Lakefront

DuSable Museum of African American History ↓

Shopping

Chicago's shops can excite the purchasing passions of the entire Midwest while surprising and delighting visitors from much farther afield. The upscale malls and shops on and around the Magnificent Mile attest to the international nature of the city, while the plethora of smaller independent boutiques shows that the city has retained its own character against the onslaught of globalized retailing.

Shopping Streets

For designer clothing, the Magnificent Mile is the showplace of Chicago. Men and women in pursuit of quality attire will find most major names represented in the high-rise malls along Michigan Avenue. For those who prefer a more personal shopping experience, a stroll around nearby Oak Street finds a clutch of elegant boutiques offering European haute couture and eager sales assistants. The same area hosts many of the city's major art galleries and antiques dealers. Venture out into the city's neighborhoods, and you'll find small, chic, funky and eco-friendly boutiques.

Antiques and Retro

More fine art and antiques dealers can be found in River North, while their brasher, funkier counterparts are a feature in the shopping districts of Andersonville, Lincoln Square and Wicker Park. There is also an abundance of outlets for clothing, both new and vintage, and places to purchase a vast range of household furnishings, often made by local craftspeople.

ENTERTAINMENT IN MALLS

Many downtown Chicago malls are more than just places to shop. They also have entertainment. The Water Tower Place mall has a Chicago Sports Museum on its top floor, and the Block 37 mall, on State Street, houses an AMC movie theater. The Shops at 900 N. Michigan Avenue have three high-end spas and a fitness center within the mall.

Chicago offers a range of shopping experiences, from designer names to smaller

Souvenirs

Simple souvenirs can be found at the Magnificent Mile stores, but more choices at better prices can be found among the touristy shops of Navy Pier. Besides miniatures of high-rise buildings, such as Willis Tower, you can snatch up T-shirts, and local, handmade gifts bearing images of the skyline seen from Lake Michigan. Quirkier items, like a "Bean" bottle opener or an Al Capone license plate, can be found at the Accent Chicago store on the top floor of Water Tower Place (▷ 75).

Tasty Reminders

Sausages might seem an unlikely reminder of Chicago but the city has been shaped by people of Eastern European descent, so handmade sausages, made with various meats, flavorings and spices, are a feature of many delis and restaurants. Chicago's famous deep-dish pizza also can be bought and shipped (within the US) from restaurants like Lou Malnati's and Gino's East.

Books and Music

Surviving the rising tide of international chains, Chicago retains an impressive number of independent bookstores; 57th Street in Hyde Park holds several. Likewise, the city's strong jazz and blues pedigree is represented by specialist CD and vinyl outlets often featuring new Chicago-based musicians alongside established names.

independent stores with goods for sale to suit every size of wallet

SPORTING SOUVENIRS

Chicago is a serious sports town, with several championship teams and legendary players, including basketball star Michael Jordan. The biggest hub of sports souvenir stores is around Wrigley Field. While you'll find mostly Chicago Cubs merchandise there, they also sell T-shirts and jerseys of other local and national teams. The city's most popular teams are the Cubs and White Sox (baseball), the Blackhawks (hockey), the Bulls (basketball) and the Bears (American football).

Shopping by Theme

Whether you're looking for a department store, a quirky boutique or something in between, you'll find it all in Chicago. On this page shops are listed by theme. For a more detailed write-up, see the individual listings in Chicago by Area.

Accessories
The Alley (▷ 103)

Art and Antiques
Arts & Artisans (▷ 33)
Bari Zaki Studio (▷ 103)
Blick Art Materials
   (▷ 33)
Broadway Antiques
   Market (▷ 103)
P.O.S.H. (▷ 75)
Poster Plus (▷ 34)
Randolph Street Market
   (▷ panel, 74)

Books and Stationery
After-Words Bookstore
   (▷ 33)
Chicago Architecture
   Center (▷ 33)
Graham Crackers Comics
   (▷ 33)
Semicolon (▷ 75)
Unabridged Bookstore
   (▷ 103)
Volumes Books (▷ 75)
Women & Children First
   Bookstore (▷ 103)

Clothes and Shoes
Azeeza (▷ 74)
Hazel Apparel and Gifts
   (▷ 103)
Ikram (▷ 74)
Matty & Lou (▷ 99)
Moon Voyage (▷ 99)
P.45 (▷ 99)
Saint Alfred (▷ 103)
Syd Jerome (▷ 34)
Una Mae's (▷ 99)
Wolfbait & B-Girls
   (▷ 103)

Home
Elements (▷ 74)
Neighborly (▷ 99)

Malls and Department Stores
900 North Michigan
   Shops (▷ 74)
The Jeweler's Center
   (▷ 33)
Macy's (▷ 34)
Navy Pier (▷ 75)
Shops at the Mart
   (▷ 75)
Water Tower Place
   (▷ 75)

Miscellaneous
American Girl Place
   (▷ 74)
Apple (▷ 74)
Art Institute of Chicago
   Museum Shop
   (▷ 33)
Atlas Stationers (▷ 33)
Enjoy Lincoln Square
   (▷ 103)
Garrett Popcorn
   (▷ panel, 34)
Kokorokoko (▷ 74)
Lego Store (▷ 75)
Merz Downtown (▷ 34)
Paperish Mess (▷ 99)
Vosges Haut Chocolat
   (▷ 34)
Whimsical Candy (▷ 34)

Chicago by Night

After sunset, much of the Magnificent Mile (▷ 68) and parts of the Loop are bathed in twinkling lights. The Wrigley Building (▷ 72), seen from Michigan Avenue Bridge, is famously stunning, while the illuminated profile of 875 N. Michigan Avenue, formerly the John Hancock Center, makes the building seem taller. From 360 CHICAGO (▷ 58–59), or the Willis Tower (▷ 28–29), a nighttime viewing reveals the grid-style patterns of city neighborhoods stretching into the distance and the deep blackness of Lake Michigan dotted by the lights of ships.

Warm Nights

Warm nights during spring, summer and fall find Chicagoans outdoors, making the most of bars and restaurants with patios and rooftops. With its hotels and late-opening shops, the Magnificent Mile is lively after dark. The updated 1.25-mile (2km) Chicago Riverwalk (▷ 30), spanning from Lake Shore Drive to Lake Street, is a pedestrian-friendly path lined with restaurants and seating areas and makes it easy to enjoy the city's skyline. More commercially oriented nightlife is found amid the theme bars and clubs of River North (▷ 60–61). The cool breezes and live music at Navy Pier (▷ 64–65) make a summertime stroll a must.

Winter Wonders

The winter period marks a high point in the city's cultural calendar with the classical concert, opera and ballet seasons fully into their stride, as well as a complete program of theater, rock and pop music.

There are plenty of clubs and theaters to keep visitors entertained after dark

CHICAGO BLUES

The former Chess Records recording studio, where some of the biggest names in blues recorded their songs, was converted into Willie Dixon's Blues Heaven Foundation (www.bluesheaven.com), a small blues museum that pays homage to the genre's history and music. It occasionally hosts small, free, top-notch concerts.

Where to Eat

Chicago is a city of hearty appetites, guaranteeing you a good meal whether at a local hot-dog stand or at a marquee restaurant. Headquarters to the nation's slaughterhouses in the 19th century, Chicago is famed for its steak houses, such as the iconic Gibson's Bar and Steakhouse, and beef sandwich stands. It's now also a leader in fine dining, with celebrated meals from top chefs Rick Bayless (Frontera Grill and Topolobampo), Stephanie Izard (Girl and the Goat, Little Goat Diner), and next-generation culinary experimenter Grant Achatz (Alinea and Next).

Ethnic Eats
Immigrant neighborhoods of Poles, Indians, Vietnamese, Chinese and Italians, among others, lay their tables richly with authentic homeland foods; visit Milwaukee Avenue for Polish borscht, Devon Street for Indian dal, Argyle Street for Vietnamese pho, Greektown's Halsted Street for saganaki or Chinatown for dim sum. Tasty and often thrifty adventures with myriad dining choices line those streets.

Deep-Dish Pizza
Chicago's famous deep-dish pizza consists of a pie-shaped pizza crust filled with mozzarella cheese, your choice of meat and vegetables, and topped with a heaping amount of Italian-flavored tomato sauce. Unlike New York-styled pizza, which is thin and flat, a single slice of deep-dish pizza can be a meal in itself.

CHICAGO-STYLE HOT DOGS
Chicago-style hot dogs are sold in hundreds of restaurants across the city. To eat one like a true Chicagoan, you must never put ketchup on it. Instead, find a restaurant that sells Vienna Beef brand hot dogs and order it with mustard, bright green relish, chopped onions, tomatoes, a pickle and sport peppers. Plus celery salt. Eat it on a steamed poppy-seed bun and with a side of french fries—where ketchup *is* allowed.

Dine at one of the city's superb restaurants or try Chicago's famed deep-dish pizza

Where to Eat by Cuisine

There are plenty of places to eat to suit all tastes and budgets in Chicago. On this page they are listed by cuisine. For a more detailed description of each restaurant, see Chicago by Area.

Asian
Arun's (▷ 106)
Phoenix (▷ 94)

Contemporary American
Alinea (▷ 78)
Atwood (▷ 37)
Field Bistro (▷ 54)
Fisk & Co. (▷ 37)
Girl & The Goat (▷ 106)
Heaven on Seven (▷ 37)
Park Grill (▷ 54)
The Signature Room at The 95th (▷ 80)
Terzo Piano (▷ 54)
The Walnut Room (▷ 38)

East European
Russian Tea Time (▷ 38)

Eclectic
Carnivale (▷ 37)
Flo & Santos (▷ 94)
Tanta (▷ 80)

French
Brindille (▷ 78)
Everest (▷ 37)
La Petite Folie (▷ 94)

German
The Berghoff (▷ 37)

Indian
Hema's Kitchen (▷ panel, 106)
Tiffin (▷ panel, 106)

Italian
Eataly (▷ 78)
Gino's East (▷ panel, 80)
Giordano's (▷ panel, 80)
The Italian Village Restaurants (▷ 38)
Maggiano's Little Italy (▷ 79)
Pizzeria Uno (▷ panel, 80)
Rosebud on Rush (▷ 80)
Spiaggia (▷ 80)

Mediterranean
The Purple Pig (▷ 79)

Mexican
5 Rabanitos Restaurante & Taquieria (▷ 94)
Frontera Grill/Topolobampo (▷ 79)
Xoco (▷ 80)

Middle Eastern
Galit (▷ 106)
Noon-o-Kabab (▷ 106)
Oasis Café (▷ 38)

Quick Bites
3 Arts Club Café (▷ 78)
Byron's Hot Dogs (▷ panel, 79)
Chicago's Home of Chicken and Waffles (▷ 94)
Eggy's Diner (▷ 54)
Goddess and the Baker (▷ 37)
Lou Mitchell's (▷ 38)
Manny's Deli & Cafeteria (▷ 94)
Meli Café (▷ 79)
Portillo's Hot Dogs & Barnelli's Salad Bowl (▷ 38)
Revival Food Hall (▷ 38)
Soundings Café (▷ 54)
Starbucks Reserve Roastery (▷ 80)
Sweet Maple Café (▷ 94)

Seafood
Brown Bag Seafood Co. (▷ 54)
GT Fish & Oyster (▷ 79)
Riva (▷ 79)

Steak, Ribs and Chops
Gibson's Bar & Steakhouse (▷ 79)
Smoque BBQ (▷ 106)
Tango Sur (▷ 106)

Vegan
Chicago Diner (▷ panel, 38)
Kal'ish (▷ panel, 38)

Top Tips For...

These great suggestions will help you tailor your ideal visit to Chicago, no matter how you choose to spend your time. Each suggestion has a fuller write-up elsewhere in the book.

ENTERTAINING THE KIDS

See the dolphin show at the Shedd Aquarium (▷ 48).
Hit Navy Pier (▷ 64) for the Children's Museum, the 196ft-high (60m) Centennial Ferris Wheel.
Make the acquaintance of Sue the T. rex at the Field Museum (▷ 46).
Visit the primates at Lincoln Park Zoo (▷ 62).

OGLING THE ARCHITECTURE

Trek to Frank Lloyd Wright's Home and Studio (▷ 100).
Take the Chicago Architecture Foundation Center River Cruise to see the city from the water with the Chicago Architecture Center (▷ 24).
Tour the Robie House (▷ 91).
Visit the Glessner House (▷ 87).

SAVING MONEY

Venture out into Chicago's neighborhoods, where you'll find budget-friendly and delicious food from around the world (▷ 106).
Ride the El for a budget skyline tour (▷ 26).
Go to Lincoln Park Zoo (▷ 62) for a second good reason—it's free.
Catch a band outdoors at Navy Pier's beer garden (▷ 64) or in Millennium Park's Pritzker Pavilion (▷ 50), also free.

SHOW GOING

Get tickets to a performance at the Goodman Theatre (▷ 36) in the Loop.
Spot the celebs on stage at the Steppenwolf Theatre (▷ 78).
Laugh it up at Second City (▷ 67), which has been open for more than 60 years.

Clockwise from top left: Navy Pier; Cindy's; take a trip on the river to view the city's architecture; go see a show or visit

DINING WITH A VIEW

Reserve a table at Everest (▷ 37) for western views.

Enjoy a drink amid the skyline at BAR 94 (at 360 CHICAGO) on the 94th floor of 875 N. Michigan Avenue (formerly John Hancock Center, ▷ 58–59).

Go to NoMI, which frames the Historic Water Tower (▷ 112, Park Hyatt Chicago) from its seventh-floor perch.

Regard the Lake Michigan views from this waterfront location at Riva (▷ 79–80).

Gaze out over Millennium Park from Cindy's, the rooftop bar at the Chicago Athletic Association Hotel (▷ 112).

A NIGHT OUT

Hit the Green Mill Cocktail Lounge (▷ 104) for a live jazz set.

Get the blues at Buddy Guy's Legends (▷ 35).

Check out the local and touring acts on stage at the Metro (▷ 104).

Dance the night away at The Underground Chicago (▷ 36).

SOUVENIR SHOPPING

Visit Vosges Haut Chocolat (▷ 34) for local handmade truffles.

Try Navy Pier shops (▷ 75) for souvenirs and Chicago Police Department T-shirts.

Hit the Wrigley Field (▷ 101) region for Cubs jerseys and gifts.

FASHION WITH EDGE

Find alternative looks at The Alley (▷ 103).

Head to Saint Alfred (▷ 103) for streetwear.

Score vintage threads at Una Mae's (▷ 99).

Visit Wolfbait & B-Girls (▷ 103) for affordable locally handmade clothing.

LITERARY CHICAGO

Find American literary masters at the American Writers Museum (▷ 30).

Celebrate local authors at the city's Printers Row Lit Fest (▷ 33).

a comedy club; Wrigley Field, home to the Cubs; Chicago has good shops, like The Alley, and great restaurants

GOING GREEN

Walk the art- and architecture-filled Millennium Park (▷ 50).
Get to Grant Park (▷ 51) in the evening to see Buckingham Fountain's light show.
Visit the greenhouses of the Garfield Park Conservatory (▷ 102).
Tour Lincoln Park, home to a zoo, gardens, a conservatory and beaches (▷ 62, 71).

OUTWARD-BOUND ACTION

Ride a bike along 18 miles (29km) of lakefront trail (▷ 84).
Get in on a game of beach volleyball at the North Avenue Beach (▷ 66).
Run a race for free at a local park, held on most Saturdays with the Chicago Area Runners Association (CARA).

LOCAL FOOD

Have a hot dog topped with all the fixings at Byron's Hot Dogs (▷ panel, 79).
Line up for a high-fat breakfast at Lou Mitchell's (▷ 38).
Devour a slice or two of deep-dish pizza at Gino's East or Pizzeria Uno (▷ panel, 80).
Tuck into Italian classic dishes at Rosebud on Rush (▷ 80) or Maggiano's Little Italy (▷ 79).

HAUT HOTELS

Have high tea in Palm Court at the Drake (▷ 112).
Be pampered at the spa in the Peninsula Chicago Hotel (▷ 112).
Ogle the multimillion-dollar art collection at the Park Hyatt Chicago (▷ 112).
Swim beneath shimmering lights in the pool at the Langham Chicago (▷ 112).

HIDDEN CHICAGO

Sneak to the basement for local caramels from Whimsical Candy (▷ 34).
Walk past jewelry cases filled with gold and diamonds to Oasis Café (▷ 38).
Hit up Eggy's Diner (▷ 54) for brunch.

From top: BP Bridge, Millennium Park; Skyline bike ride; Pizza is a great option in the city; The Peninsula Chicago

The Loop

Named for the elevated train that rings the district, the downtown Loop is where Chicago does business. The historic center is also the seat of government and the oldest shopping district in the city.

Top 25

8

9

10

11

12

Chicago Riverwalk

NORTH

WEST WACKER DRIVE

NTH LASALLE

Nth Post Pl

West

Wells

North

North

North

North

State/Lake
Street

Chicago
Theatre

NTH WACKER DRIVE

NTH FRANKLIN

WEST
ST

Lake

Clark/
Lake

Clark

Dearborn

STATE

Lake

RANDOLPH STREET

LOOP

Palace
Theatre

City
Hall &
County Building

ST
Street

Street

Street

WEST WASHINGTON STREET

EAST

Civic
Opera
House

Washington/
Wells

Washington

STREET

Loop Public
Sculptures

STATE

West

Madison

STH LASALLE

Street

South

South

Washington

Mercantile
Exchange

STH FRANKLIN

El
Train

South

Monroe

Street

Clark

Street

Dearborn

Monroe

SOUTH

The Sullivan
Center

SOUTH

West

Marquette
Building

WEST ADAMS Rookery STREET

EAST

The

WEST WACKER

Willis
Tower

Quincy

West Quincy
St

Street

Federal
Office
Building

Street

STATE

Jackson

WEST JACKSON BOULEVARD

STREET

Wells

Chicago
Board of Trade

South

South

Monadnock
Building

Harold
Washington
Library

DRIVE

West
Street

Van
Buren

South
Sherman

Street

LaSalle/
Van Buren

Clark

Federal

Dearborn

East

Harold
Library

D'Angelo
Park

LaSalle

South

Plymouth

WEST CONGRESS PARKWAY

EAST

STREET

Street

LASALLE STREET
STATION

Printers
Row

STREET

P

WEST HARRISON STREET

EAST

South Wells Street

South
Sherman

LaSalle
Street

Street

Street

Street

Harrison

East

West
Street

Polk

Street

Dearborn
Station

East

0   250 m

0   250 yds

D   **E**

Chicago Architecture
Foundation Center River Cruise

EAST WACKER DRIVE

NTH

North

South

MICHIGAN

North

North

Water Street

North Stetson Avenue

Illinois
Center

East Lake Street

Wabash

Garland

American
Writers
Museum

Prudential Building

Court

Washington/
Wabash

MICHIGAN AVENUE

EAST RANDOLPH DRIVE

Ave

MILLENNIUM
STATION

WASHINGTON

Chicago
Cultural
Center

STREET

Madison/
Wabash

Madison Street

South

SOUTH

Chicago

Chicago River

Lake

Michigan

Wabash

Adams /
Wabash

MICHIGAN

ADAMS ST

Symphony
Center

Avenue

MICHIGAN AVENUE

Van Buren St

Washington
y Center

Congress

CONGRESS

PARKWAY

Plaza

Congress
Hotel

South

Harrison Street

Museum of
Contemporary
Photography

Wabash

Spertus Institute for Jewish
Learning and Leadership

Balbo Avenue

East Balbo Drive

Avenue

Merle Reskin
(Blackstone)
Theatre

8th Street

Chicago
Harbor

F

G

Chicago Architecture Foundation Center River Cruise

See the city from the Chicago River aboard a cruise boat

THE BASICS

architecture.org

✚ F9

✉ 111 E. Wacker Drive (board at dock location at Michigan Avenue and Wacker Drive)

☎ 312/922-8687

🕐 Cruises daily Mar–Nov. Closed Dec–Feb

🚇 Brown, Orange, Green, Purple, Pink and Red Lines: State/Lake

🚌 6, 121, 146, 147, 148, 151

✋ Expensive

HIGHLIGHTS

● Wrigley Building
● Marina City Towers
● 333 W. Wacker Drive
● Chicago River bridges
● Willis Tower
● Tribune Tower

The Chicago Architecture Foundation Center River Cruise Aboard Chicago's First Lady is the most in-depth, authentic architecture river cruise available. It is led by Chicago Architecture Center-certified volunteer docents who share the secrets and stories behind more than 50 significant buildings in only 90 minutes.

Architectural historians Founded by architects and preservationists in 1966 to preserve the Glessner House on Prairie Avenue, the Chicago Architecture Center has today grown into one of the largest cultural institutions in the city. Volunteer guides narrate the trip, which takes in Bertrand Goldberg's 1964 corn-cob-shape Marina City Towers, the triangular, white, tile-clad Wrigley Building erected by the chewing-gum magnate William Wrigley Jr., as well as the 1922-erected Tribune Tower. The Tribune Tower's peaks are crowned by a series of Gothic flying buttresses which were inspired by those of a French cathedral. New city landmarks include Vista Tower.

Chicago River In the 17th century, American Indians occupied the banks of the Chicago River where it flowed into Lake Michigan. Over the next centuries as the population grew, wastewater from the river flowed into Lake Michigan, contaminating the city's drinking water. So in 1900, engineers reversed the river's flow away from the lake and into the Sanitary and Ship Canal.

Loop Public Sculptures

A few blocks in Chicago's Loop district comprise an outdoor exhibition space devoted to some of the world's finest sculptors. It's ideal for those looking for a cultural self-guided walking tour.

The collection In 1967, then-mayor Richard J. Daley dedicated the monumental, untitled sculpture by Pablo Picasso at Daley Center Plaza (Dearborn and Washington streets), considered the first non-commemorative city sculpture and the start of Chicago's strong public arts program, highlighted by its collection in the Loop. Across Washington Street, Joan Miró's depiction of a woman with outstretched arms faces the Picasso. Marc Chagall's stone mosaic *The Four Seasons* is at Dearborn and Monroe streets. Two blocks down at Dearborn and Adams, Alexander Calder's graceful, neon-orange *Flamingo* contrasts with the dark-glass Federal Center. Jean Dubuffet's white fiberglass *Monument with Standing Beast* resides at the James R. Thompson Center where Clark meets Randolph Street. And just over the Chicago River in the West Loop at 600 W. Madison, Claes Oldenburg created *Batcolumn*, a 101ft (31m) steel baseball bat.

Chicago's Picasso Local architect William Hartmann convinced Pablo Picasso to create a sculpture for downtown Chicago. Picasso's untitled work, "a gift to the people of Chicago," is today part of everyday Loop life, and skateboarders launch from its sloping base.

THE BASICS

cityofchicago.org/publicart

🔠 E10

🚇 Blue, Brown, Red, Green Loop stops

🚌 20, 22

HIGHLIGHTS

● *Untitled* by Pablo Picasso
● *Flamingo* by Alexander Calder
● *Monument with Standing Beast* by Jean Dubuffet
● *Chicago* by Joan Miró
● *Batcolumn* by Claes Oldenburg
● *The Four Seasons* by Marc Chagall
● *Cloud Gate* (also known as "the Bean") by Anish Kapoor
● *Crown Fountain* by Jaume Plensa
● *Agora* by Magdalena Abakanowicz

Riding the El Train

The El Train crossing the Chicago River (left); Quincy station (right)

THE BASICS

transitchicago.com

✚ E10

☎ 888/968-7282

🕐 Mon–Sat 4.30am–1am, Sun 5am–1am

🚇 Brown Line Loop stops

🚌 29

✋ Inexpensive

HIGHLIGHTS

- Crossing the Chicago River aboard the Brown Line
- Seeing into baseball's Wrigley Field from the Addison stop on the Red Line
- Snaking around the downtown high-rises aboard the Brown Line

DID YOU KNOW?

- Blue Line, largely underground, efficiently connects O'Hare airport to downtown.
- The elevated Orange Line links Midway Airport and downtown.

One of Chicago's most distinctive symbols, the elevated train, El or L for short, provides a commuter's close-up of the city's downtown district as well as its neighborhood backyards.

Tracking history New York erected the first elevated train in 1867, a feat Chicago soon copied, with a flurry of companies devoted to the project. The first line (3.6 miles/5.8km) opened in 1892 and was nicknamed the "Alley L" for running above city-owned alleys, sparing the transit company from securing access privileges from the property owners. Expansion of the El lines was linked to many major events in Chicago history, including the World's Columbian Exposition. Independently owned rail lines agreed to link their services downtown in a "Union Loop" in 1897, the origin of the district's name. Today, Chicago Transit Authority operates eight color-coded routes over 224.1 miles (361km) of track.

Brown Line The best line for sightseers, the Brown Line circles the downtown Loop, crosses the Chicago River heading north through the neighborhoods of River North, Lincoln Park, Lakeview and Lincoln Square, before terminating at Kimball Street. Board anywhere in the Loop to weave through the high-rises two stories up from street level. Disembark at any stop, and using overhead platform bridges that connect north- and south-bound tracks without a transfer fee, return in the opposite direction.

Interior of The Rookery
building (left); detail
of the exterior of the
building (right)

TOP
25

The Rookery

Designed by Daniel Burnham and John Wellborn Root in the 1880s, and later renovated by Frank Lloyd Wright, the Rookery is among Chicago's most admired landmarks.

Birdhouse After the Great Fire of 1871, birds took to roosting in the water-storage building that was temporarily City Hall. It was consequently nicknamed the Rookery. Public feeling dictated that the building that replaced it should formally take on this name. Rising 11 floors, the Rookery was among the tallest buildings in the world on completion and one of the most important early skyscrapers. The thick, load-bearing, brick-and-granite walls at the base, decorated with Roman, Moorish and Venetian (and several rook) motifs, support upper levels with an iron frame that enabled the structure to be raised higher than previously thought possible. Due to its construct, the Rookery is considered by architectural historians to be a transitional building in the evolution of the modern skyscraper.

Interior treasures The facade, however, is scant preparation for the interior. The inner court is bathed in incredible natural light entering through a vast domed skylight. Imposing lamps hang above the floor, and Root's intricate ironwork decorates the stairways that climb up to a 360-degree balcony. The white marble, introduced by Frank Lloyd Wright in 1905, increases the sense of space and brightness.

THE BASICS

therookerybuilding.com

⊞ E10

✉ 209 S. LaSalle Street

☎ 312/553-6100

🕐 Lobby open during business hours

🚊 Brown, Orange Lines: Quincy

🚌 1, 22, 151

♿ Good

🎫 Free

HIGHLIGHTS

● Light-flooded, glass-roofed inner court
● Ten-story spiral staircase
● Prairie-style light fixtures
● External terra-cotta ornamentation
● Carrara marble walls
● Mosaic tile floors

THE LOOP TOP 25

Willis Tower

HIGHLIGHTS

- Visibility of up to 50 miles (80km) on a clear day
- Standing on The Ledge and daring to look down
- Feeling the building sway
- High-powered telescopes
- Sunset views after 4pm

DID YOU KNOW?

- Six robotic window washers mounted on the roof clean all the 16,000 windows.
- Elevators soar up to 1,600ft (487m) per minute.

The Willis Tower (previously known as the Sears Tower until 2009), rises higher than any other structure in the city. As well as sleek and stylish architecture, it has the highest man-made vantage point in the western hemisphere and the vertigo-inducing Ledge.

Built from tubes From 1974 to 1996, the Willis Tower's 110 floors and 1,454ft (443m) height made it the tallest building in the world, rising from the Loop with a distinctive profile of black aluminum and bronze-tinted glass. Architect Bruce Graham, of Skidmore, Owings & Merrill, structured it around nine 75sq-ft (7sq-m) bundled tubes, which decline in number as the building reaches upward. Aside from increasing the colossal structure's strength, this technique

Clockwise from top left: A most amazing view down from The Ledge; the view from the Skydeck at the Willis Tower; a 99th-floor event space; people look out over Chicago from The Ledge

also echoes the stepback, New York skyscraper style of the late 1920s. Among the early tasks during the three-year construction was the creation of foundation supports capable of holding a 222,500-ton building. The two rooftop antennae were added in 1982, increasing the building's height by 253ft (77m). Sears, the retail company that commissioned the building of the tower, moved out in 1992.

Seeing for miles The 103rd-floor Skydeck is accessible via a 70-second elevator ride, and reveals an invigorating panorama of the city. Step out onto The Ledge, a 1.5in (3.8cm) thick glass-bottomed window extension that lets you look straight down to the city streets and river 1,353ft (412m) below—not recommended if you have a fear of heights.

THE BASICS

theskydeck.com

⊞ D10

✉ 103rd floor, 233 S. Wacker Drive

☎ 312/875-9696

🕐 Skydeck: Mar–Sep daily 9am–10pm; Oct–Feb 10–8. Last entry 30 mins before closing. May be closed in high winds

🍴 Restaurants and cafés

Ⓠ Brown, Orange, Pink Lines: Quincy

🚌 1, 7, 28, 126, 151, 156

♿ Excellent

✋ Moderate

More to See

AMERICAN WRITERS MUSEUM

americanwritersmuseum.org
This first-of-its-kind national museum, which opened in May 2017, celebrates American writers such as Kurt Vonnegut, Mark Twain and Gwendolyn Brooks. Artifacts from the writers' homes are on display, as well as interactive, high-tech exhibits that explain each writer's influence on US culture.

➕ F9 ✉ 180 N. Michigan Avenue, 2nd Floor ☎ 312/374-8790 🕐 Daily 10–5 🚇 Brown, Green, Pink, Purple Lines: Randolph/Wabash; Red Line: Lake 🚌 143, 146, 151 ♿ Good 💵 Expensive

CHICAGO CULTURAL CENTER

chicagoculturalcenter.org
The Washington Street entrance leads through hefty bronze doors into the lobby, whose grand staircase is bordered by mosaics set into white marble balustrades. The second floor has the hall and rotunda of the Great Army of the Republic, with Tennessee marble walls and a mosaic tile floor, while the floor above holds the Preston Bradley Hall, with a Tiffany-glass dome. The main exhibition hall on the top level features columns that rise to meet a coffered ceiling. A number of free exhibits, performances and events occur year-round.

➕ F9 ✉ 78 E. Washington Street ☎ 312/744-6630 🕐 Mon–Fri 9–7, Sat–Sun 10–5 🚇 Brown, Orange Lines: Madison; Red: Lake; Blue: Washington 🚌 3, 4, 60, 66, 147, 151

CHICAGO RIVERWALK

The Chicago Riverwalk is a thriving and bustling area, perfect for those wanting to enjoy a walk or jog or just sit back and watch the boats float along the Chicago River. It's easy to grab a drink or dinner at one of the many restaurants and bars that line the trail.

➕ E9 ✉ Banks of Chicago River, beneath Wacker Drive, between Lake Shore Drive and Lake Street 🚇 Brown, Green, Red, Pink, Purple Lines: State/Lake; Blue Line: Clark/Lake 🚌 151 ♿ Good 💵 Free

HAROLD WASHINGTON LIBRARY CENTER

chipublib.org/locations/34/
Chicago's main library, named after the city's first African American mayor, has four massive owls at each corner of the building, said to represent growth and wisdom.

➕ E11 ✉ 400 S. State Street ☎ 312/747-4300 🕐 Mon–Thu 9–9, Fri–Sat 9–5, Sun 1–5 🚇 Brown, Orange, Pink Lines: HW Library; Blue Line: Jackson 🚌 6, 29, 146 ♿ Good

MARQUETTE BUILDING

marquette.macfound.org
Completed in 1895, this building is among the unsung masterpieces of Chicago architecture. It displays the

Chicago Cultural Center

first use of the three-part "Chicago window"—plate glass spans the width between the building's steel supports. Lobby reliefs record the expedition of French Jesuit missionary Jacques Marquette; the entrance doors' panther heads are by Edward Kemeys, also responsible for the lions fronting the Art Institute of Chicago (▷ 44). ✚ E10 ✉ 140 S. Dearborn Street ◷ Daily 7am–10pm 🚇 Brown, Orange Lines: Quincy

PRINTERS ROW
The industrial buildings lining Dearborn Street were the core of Chicago's printing industry during the late 19th century. Many are now loft-style apartments, with galleries, shops and restaurants. ✚ E11 ✉ Dearborn Street 🚇 Blue Line: LaSalle; Red Line: Harrison 🚌 22, 62

SPERTUS INSTITUTE FOR JEWISH LEARNING AND LEADERSHIP
spertus.edu
The Spertus Institute hosts films, concerts and exhibitions focused on Jewish wisdom and culture. It's housed within an environmentally sustainable building with a 10-story faceted glass facade made of 726 individual pieces of glass in 556 different shapes. The space includes classrooms, the Asher Library and a 400-seat theater. ✚ F11 ✉ 610 S. Michigan Avenue ☎ 312/322-1700 ◷ Museum: Mon–Wed 9–5, Thu 9–6, Fri 9–3, Sun 10–5 🚇 Red Line: Harrison 🚌 1, 3, 4, 7, 26, 147 ♿ Good 💰 Moderate

THE SULLIVAN CENTER
thesullivancenter.com
The elaborately decorated exterior of the former Carson Pirie Scott Building was created by architect Louis Sullivan over a five-year period beginning in 1899. Vast pieces of glass span the entire width of the building. The Sullivan Center houses retail and office space and The School of the Art Institute of Chicago. ✚ F10 ✉ 1 S. State Street ☎ 312/940-2070 🚇 Blue, Red Lines: Monroe 🚌 6, 29, 36, 146, 147 ♿ Good 💰 Free

Marquette Building

Corner entrance to the Sullivan Center

Loop the Loop

The best way to see the many architectural and artistic highlights of the Loop is to walk from point to point.

DISTANCE: 2 miles (3km) **ALLOW:** 60–90 minutes

START

WILLIS TOWER (▷ 28) D10
Brown, Orange Lines: Quincy

❶ Begin at Willis Tower (1974), until 1996 the world's tallest building, with a fantastic view from its 103rd-floor Skydeck.

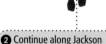

❷ Continue along Jackson Boulevard for the Chicago Board of Trade (1930), one of the city's finest art-deco skyscrapers.

❸ Turn north on LaSalle Street and peek into the architecturally stunning Rookery (▷ 27). Continue north to the junction with Washington Street.

❹ Turn east on Washington to the Daley Center Plaza, on the north side between Clark and Dearborn, to view downtown's 50ft- (15m-) tall Picasso sculpture (▷ 25).

❺ Cross the street to view Miró's sculpture, *Chicago* (▷ 25), marking the plaza of 69 W. Washington Street.

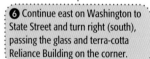

❻ Continue east on Washington to State Street and turn right (south), passing the glass and terra-cotta Reliance Building on the corner.

❼ Continue to Louis Sullivan's early 20th-century Sullivan Center (▷ 31). Walk west on Monroe to Dearborn, then one block south for the Marquette Building (1895; ▷ 30).

❽ Stroll east on Adams, then north along Michigan Avenue to the Chicago Cultural Center (1897), at the junction with Washington Street.

END

CHICAGO CULTURAL CENTER (▷ 30)
F9 Brown, Orange Lines: Madison

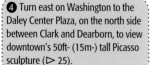

Shopping

AFTER-WORDS BOOKSTORE

after-wordschicago.com

A great independent bookstore: Stacks of new and used titles fill the shelves upstairs and in the basement of this unassuming locale off the main drag.

✚ F8 ✉ 23 E. Illinois Street ☎ 312/464-1110 🚇 Red Line: Grand 🚌 3, 29, 65, 146, 147

ART INSTITUTE OF CHICAGO MUSEUM SHOP

shop.artic.edu

This outstanding gallery shop features a range of fashions including scarves, tote bags and original jewelry, stationery, home furnishings, lamps, sculpture, decorative and fine art, as well as a selection of books about art and artists.

✚ F10 ✉ 111 S. Michigan Ave ☎ 855/301-9612 🚇 Blue, Red Lines: Monroe; Brown, Orange, Pink, Green Lines: Adams 🚌 3, 4, 6, 7, 147, 151

ARTS & ARTISANS

artsartisans.com

For one-of-a-kind gifts, visit this family-run store selling contemporary American crafts, art and jewelry. There are three other locations in the downtown area.

✚ F9 ✉ 35 E. Wacker Drive ☎ 312/578-0126 🚇 Brown, Green, Orange, Pink, Purple Lines: State/Lake 🚌 6, 146, 147, 151

ATLAS STATIONERS

atlasstationers.com

This old-school family-run stationery shop features everything from fountain pens to furniture and thousands more items to meet the needs of locals and visitors alike. In business since 1939, it's now being run by third- and fourth-generation family members.

✚ E9 ✉ 227 W. Lake Street ☎ 312/726-5261 🚇 Blue, Brown, Orange Lines: Clark/Lake 🚌 37, 156

BLICK ART MATERIALS

dickblick.com

Art supply store Blick stocks everything from oil paints to sculptor's clay. Sketchpads and kids' projects may appeal to travelers.

✚ F10 ✉ 42 S. State Street ☎ 312/920-0300 🚇 Red Line: Madison State; Blue Line: Monroe 🚌 29, 146, 147

CHICAGO ARCHITECTURE CENTER

architecture.org

An exemplary source of books on architecture, as well as clever, colorful gifts that make tasteful souvenirs.

✚ F9 ✉ 111 E. Wacker Drive ☎ 312/922-3432 🚇 Blue: Clark/Lake; Brown, Orange, Pink, Green: State/Lake; Red: Lake 🚌 3, 4, 6, 146, 147, 151, 157

GRAHAM CRACKERS COMICS

grahamcrackers.com

This well-stocked comic-book store appeals to the area's college students and comic aficionados.

✚ F10 ✉ 77 E. Madison Street ☎ 312/629-1810 🚇 Red Line: Munroe 🚌 29

THE JEWELER'S CENTER

jewelerscenter.com

More than 180 jewelers sell fine jewelry and one-of-a-kind estate pieces across

PRINTERS ROW LIT FEST

To celebrate this district's history in all things print production, Chicago's annual Printers Row Lit Fest (printersrowlitfest.org), held over a weekend in early June, lures new, used and antiques book-sellers to temporary shops that are erected under tents lining South Dearborn between Congress and Polk. Event programs may include author readings, signings and discussions.

GARRETT POPCORN

People line up for blocks to buy the CaramelCrisp, CheeseCorn and butter versions of this popcorn, which is popular with tourists and celebrities. Mix a few of your favorite types together in a bag, box or decorative tin. They have eight locations downtown, including Navy Pier. To find out more visit garrettpopcorn.com.

13 floors of this beautiful structure built in 1912. Also on offer are custom-designed rings.

🚉 F10 ✉ 5 S. Wabash Avenue ☎ 312/853-2057 🚊 Brown, Orange, Green, Pink Lines: Washington/Wabash 🚌 20, 56, 60, 124, 157

MACY'S

visitmacyschicago.com

Once home to the beloved Marshall Field's department store, the New York-based Macy's chain has retained many of the old store's famous features, including the century-old green clock that hangs outside. Inside, the store sells clothing, home goods and jewelry. It also has several restaurants, including the legendary Walnut Room (▷ 38).

🚉 F10 ✉ 111 N. State Street ☎ 312/781-1000 🚊 Red Line: State; Blue Line: Washington 🚌 29, 36, 146, 147

MERZ DOWNTOWN

merzapothecary.com

Located within the historic Palmer House Hotel, this apothecary is filled with make-up, pampering supplies and a range of homeopathic remedies. The European-style original location, which dates back to 1875, can be found in Lincoln Square.

🚉 F10 ✉ 17 E. Monroe Street ☎ 312/781-6900 🚊 Brown, Orange, Pink, Green Lines: Adams/Wabash 🚌 29, 146, 147

POSTER PLUS

posterplus.com

Head here for historic posters, mostly celebrating landmarks in Chicago and US history, though many are attractive reprints rather than originals.

🚉 F11 ✉ 30 E. Adams Street ☎ 312/461-9277 🚊 Blue, Red Lines: Monroe; Brown, Orange, Pink, Green Lines: Adams 🚌 3, 4, 6, 7, 147, 151

SYD JEROME

sydjerome.com

Esquire magazine once rated this upscale men's store "Best in Class" for its impeccably stylish fashions coming from the likes of Armani, Hickey Freeman and John Varvatos.

🚉 E10 ✉ 20 N. Clark Street ☎ 312/346-0333 🚊 Brown, Orange, Pink, Purple Lines: Washington/Wells 🚌 22, 24, 36

VOSGES HAUT CHOCOLAT

vosgeschocolate.com

Local chocolatier Katrina Markoff has created a cult-like following for her truffles, many of which feature indigenous spices, flowers, roots and herbs. They are not inexpensive, but they are definitely delicious.

🚉 F8 ✉ Northbridge Mall, 520 N. Michigan Avenue ☎ 312/644-9450 🚊 Red Line: Grand 🚌 3, 29, 65, 146, 147, 151, 157

WHIMSICAL CANDY

whimsicalcandy.com

Hidden in the basement and down the hall is this adorable kitchen that makes caramels, marshmallows and an assortment of candy bars daily. Visitors are welcome to stop by and see the action or take a class.

🚉 E9 ✉ 175 N. Franklin, Lower Level ☎ 312/781-0053 🚊 Blue, Brown, Orange Lines: Clark/Lake 🚌 37

Entertainment and Nightlife

AIRE ANCIENT BATHS

beaire.com

Located adjacent to the Loop in River North, this restored factory from 1902 is a bath house like you've never seen.
🚇 C7 ✉️ 800 W. Superior Street ☎️ 312/945-7414 🚊 Blue Line: Grand 🚌 8, 66

AUDITORIUM THEATRE

auditoriumtheatre.org

Designed by the revered Adler & Sullivan, the marvelously renovated Auditorium Building is a fine venue for dance, music and drama productions.
🚇 F11 ✉️ 50 E. Ida B. Wells Drive
☎️ 312/341-2310 🚊 Red Line: Harrison
🚌 3, 4, 6, 126, 147

BUDDY GUY'S LEGENDS

buddyguy.com

Co-owner and famed blues guitarist Buddy Guy presents outstanding blues acts, including internationally known names and local rising stars.
🚇 F11 ✉️ 700 S. Wabash Avenue
☎️ 312/427-1190 🚊 Red Line: Harrison
🚌 3, 4, 6

CADILLAC PALACE THEATRE

cadillacpalacetheatre.com

One of Chicago's major theaters set along Randolph Street, comprising the Loop's theater district, the Cadillac Palace is often booked by big Broadway touring companies.

COMEDY SHOWS

A Chicago theater staple, *Late Nite Catechism* (✉️ Royal George Theatre, 1641 N. Halsted ☎️ 312/988-9000) is a hilarious, interactive one-woman show on Saturday and Sunday. During *Bible Bingo*, audience members actually play games of bingo on Fridays and Saturdays at 8pm.

🚇 E9 ✉️ 151 W. Randolph Street
☎️ 312/977-1700 🚊 Brown, Orange Lines: Washington 🚌 20, 56, 60, 124, 157

CHICAGO THEATRE

msg.com/the-chicago-theatre

The 3,600-seat, French baroque-style Chicago Theatre, with the classic vertical C-H-I-C-A-G-O spelled out on the marquee, hosts concert tours in rock, jazz, hip-hop and ballet, as well as limited-run theater productions.
🚇 F9 ✉️ 175 N. State Street ☎️ 800/745-3000 🚊 Red Line: Lake 🚌 29, 36

CIBC THEATRE

banktheaterchicago.com

This handsome place is a rare reminder that theater once thrived in the Loop. It is best known for its musicals.
🚇 F10 ✉️ 18 W. Monroe Street ☎️ 312/977-1700, 800/775-2000 🚊 Blue and Red Lines: Monroe 🚌 22, 24, 36, 62, 151

CIVIC OPERA HOUSE

civicoperahouse.com

The distinguished Lyric Opera of Chicago company perform from late September to the end of March at this art-deco auditorium (also one of the main dance venues). Seats are sometimes available at the box office on the day of the performance.
🚇 D10 ✉️ 20 N. Wacker Drive ☎️ 312/332-2244 🚊 Brown, Orange Lines: Washington/Wells 🚌 20

GENE SISKEL FILM CENTER

siskelfilmcenter.org

The School of the Arts Institute of Chicago runs this ambitious cinema named for a former, highly influential film critic. There are two screens showing foreign, independent and vintage films in repertory.

➕ F9 ✉ 164 N. State Street ☎ 312/846-2800 🚇 Red Line: Lake 🚌 29, 36

GOODMAN THEATRE

goodmantheatre.org

The Goodman Theatre hosts some of the best drama in the city, including both classics and cutting-edge contemporary productions. Well-known actors including Brian Dennehy and Marcia Gay Harden have performed here and lauded playwrights August Wilson and Arthur Miller debuted plays here.

➕ E9 ✉ 170 N. Dearborn Street ☎ 312/443-3800 🚇 Blue Line: Washington 🚌 22, 36

JAMES M. NEDERLANDER THEATRE

broadwayinchicago.com

Formerly known as the Oriental Theatre, this performance space presents first-rate shows.

➕ E9 ✉ 24 W. Randolph Street ☎ 312/977-1700 🚇 Red Line: Lake; Blue Line: Washington 🚌 22, 24, 36, 62

ROOF ON THE WIT

roofonthewit.com

Often ranked as one of the city's best rooftop bars, the ROOF is known for its far-reaching views of downtown Chicago. Enjoy music by world-renowned DJs and acoustic music series from 27 stories above, complete with stunning skyline views.

➕ F9 ✉ 201 N. State Street ☎ 312/239-9502 🚇 Brown, Orange, Green Lines: State/Lake; Red Line: Lake 🚌 2, 29, 146

SILK ROAD RISING

silkroadrising.org

Located in the historic Chicago Temple building, this young company is known for showing works by playwrights of Asian, Middle Eastern and Mediterranean descent.

➕ E10 ✉ 77 W. Washington Street ☎ 312/857-1234 🚇 Red Line: Lake; Blue Line: Washington 🚌 19, 22, 24

SYMPHONY CENTER

cso.org

From September to May the renowned Chicago Symphony Orchestra (CSO) is in residence in this sumptuous Greek Revival hall, built in 1904. Tickets are sold early, but some may be available on the day of performance. On-site Opus Restaurant and Café offers three-course prix-fixe dinners at two seatings on concert dates.

➕ F10 ✉ 220 S. Michigan Avenue ☎ 312/294-3000 🚇 Brown, Orange and Green Lines: Adams 🚌 3, 4, 26, 143, 147

THE UNDERGROUND CHICAGO

theundergroundchicago.com

This late-night club features some of the country's top DJs. Celebrities often drop in, as do local Chicago athletes, and mingle with the well-dressed crowd. The club has two spaces—a high-energy, modern dance club area, and an old-school, upscale lounge with plush seating. Doors open around 10pm, Wednesday to Sunday.

➕ D8 ✉ 56 W. Illinois Street ☎ 312/644-7600 🚇 Red Line: Grand 🚌 22, 36, 65

HALF-PRICE TICKETS

Hot Tix (✉ 72 E. Randolph Street or 108 N. State Street) offers half-price tickets for many of the day's theater events. A website (hottix.org) lists the day's performances. Full-price advance tickets are also available from Hot Tix, as well as from Ticketmaster (☎ 312/559-1212).

Where to Eat

ATWOOD ($$)

atwoodrestaurant.com

In the evening, dine here on foods such as pork chops and pan-roasted chicken. Café staples including salads and soups lighten up the lunch fare at this window-wrapped restaurant.

⊞ E9 ✉ 1 W. Washington Street
☎ 312/368-1900 🕐 Daily breakfast, lunch and dinner 🚇 Red Line: Washington 🚌 29

THE BERGHOFF ($$)

theberghoff.com

A direct descendant of one of Chicago's most fondly remembered restaurants, the historic Berghoff serves classic German fare such as *spätzleknödel* and *Wiener schnitzel* in an old world-inspired room with stained-glass accents. Stop at the café for lunchtime sandwiches including *sauerbraten*.

⊞ E10 ✉ 17 W. Adams Street ☎ 312/427-3170 🕐 Mon–Sat lunch and dinner 🚇 Red Line: Jackson 🚌 1, 7, 28, 126, 151

CARNIVALE ($$$)

carnivalechicago.com

Located in the West Loop, this colorfully decorated and fun restaurant serves dishes from South America, Spain and the Caribbean for brunch, lunch, dinner and happy-hour guests.

⊞ D11 ✉ 702 W. Fulton Market
☎ 312/850-5005 🕐 Dinner Mon–Sat, brunch and lunch Sun 🚇 Green, Pink Lines: Clinton 🚌 8, 56

EVEREST ($$$$)

everestrestaurant.com

This 40th-floor top-notch restaurant that commands far-reaching views—beloved of financial wheeler-dealers—offers an inspiring look at chef Jean Joho's native Alsace. The restaurant's Loop location, prices and standards of cooking are all breathtakingly high.

⊞ E10 ✉ 425 S. Financial Place ☎ 312/663-8920 🕐 Dinner only; closed Sun, Mon 🚇 Blue Line: LaSalle 🚌 22, 24, 36

FISK & CO. ($$$)

fiskandcochicago.com

A rotating selection of oysters from the raw bar, burgers and craft beer are served at Fisk & Co., located inside Hotel Monaco.

⊞ F9 ✉ 225 N. Wabash Avenue ☎ 312/236-9300 🕐 Mon–Fri breakfast, lunch and dinner, Sat–Sun breakfast, brunch and dinner 🚇 Red Line: Lake; Brown, Green, Orange Lines: State 🚌 120, 121, 134, 135, 136

GODDESS AND THE BAKER ($)

goddessandthebaker.com

A breezy, natural, light-filled, fast-casual café that serves up breakfast, fresh sandwiches, salads, baked goods and coffee all day long.

⊞ E9 ✉ 225 N. LaSalle Street ☎ 312/374-3625 🕐 Daily breakfast and lunch 🚇 Blue, Brown, Orange, Purple, Pink and Green Lines: Clark/Lake 🚌 134, 135, 136, 156

HEAVEN ON SEVEN ($$)

heavenonseven.com

Chef Jimmy Banos' menu mixes class New Orleans-style food with Creole cooking at this restaurant on the seventh floor of a building along Jewelers Row.

⊞ F9 ✉ 111 N. Wabash Avenue, 7th Floor ☎ 312/263-6443 🕐 Mon–Sat breakfast and

lunch, Thu–Sat Dinner 🚇 Brown, Green, Orange, Pink, Purple Lines: Washington/Wabash 🚌 4, 20, 66, 147 ℹ️ Cash only

THE ITALIAN VILLAGE RESTAURANTS ($$–$$$$)

italianvillage-chicago.com

Three Italians in one building: the expensive and smart Vivere, the mid-priced and seafood-focused La Cantina and the good-value, the Village.
➕ E10 ✉️ 71 W. Monroe Street ☎️ 312/332-7005 🕐 Vivere: Tue–Fri lunch, Tue–Sat dinner; La Cantina: Tue–Sat dinner only; The Village: daily lunch and dinner 🚇 Blue Line: Monroe 🚌 22, 24, 36, 62, 151

LOU MITCHELL'S ($)

loumitchellsrestaurant.com

Long-standing Chicago diner serves omelets and home-baked pastries.
➕ E9 ✉️ 565 W. Jackson Boulevard ☎️ 312/939-3111 🕐 Breakfast and lunch only 🚇 Blue Line: Clinton 🚌 7, 60, 126, 157

OASIS CAFÉ ($)

Walk past rows of jewelry cases filled with gems to find this Middle Eastern, fast-casual restaurant serving falafel and kebob sandwiches.
➕ F10 ✉️ 21 N. Wabash Avenue ☎️ 312/443-9534 🕐 Mon–Sat lunch 🚇 Brown, Orange, Purple, Green and Pink Lines: Washington/Wabash 🚌 19, 20, 56, 60, 66, 124, 157

PORTILLO'S HOT DOGS & BARNELLI'S SALAD BOWL ($)

portillos.com

This is the place to come for a real Chicago hot dog or tasty Italian beef sandwich. Order at the counter and then find a seat in the memorabilia-covered dining area.
➕ E8 ✉️ 100 W. Ontario Street

☎️ 312/587-8930 🕐 Daily lunch and dinner 🚇 Red Line: Grand 🚌 22, 125

REVIVAL FOOD HALL ($–$$)

A food marketplace featuring 15 of Chicago's neighborhood restaurants. Choose your dishes and eat your meal on the first floor of a historic building.
➕ E10 ✉️ 125 S. Clark Street ☎️ 773/999-9411 🕐 Mon–Fri breakfast, lunch and dinner 🚇 Blue Line: Monroe 🚌 22, 24, 36, 62, 151

RUSSIAN TEA TIME ($$)

russianteatime.com

You'll hear Balalaika music playing in this atmospheric, wood-covered room with red leather booths. The menu features haerty food but so is caviar and other Russian specialties.
➕ F10 ✉️ 77 E. Adams Street ☎️ 312/360-0000 🕐 Daily lunch, dinner and afternoon tea 🚇 Brown, Orange, Purple, Green and Pink Lines: Adams/Wabash 🚌 3, 4, 6, 26, 143

THE WALNUT ROOM ($$$)

macysrestaurants.com/walnut-room

A Chicago tradition since 1905, this world-famous restaurant was the first ever city eatery to open for service in a department store.
➕ F9 ✉️ 111 N. State Street ☎️ 312/781-3139 🕐 Tue–Sat lunch and dinner, Sun–Mon lunch 🚇 Blue Line: Washington; Red Line: State 🚌 2, 29, 146, 148

FOR VEGANS

Most Chinese, Thai and Vietnamese restaurants offer meat-free versions of their staples, as do Indian eateries; Italian restaurants are another possibility. For vegan restaurant options, try Chicago Diner (✉️ 3411 N. Halsted Street ☎️ 773/935-6696) and Kal'ish (✉️ 1313 W. Wilson Avenue ☎️ 773/293-7768).

Museum Campus

The 57-acre (23ha) lakefront Museum Campus encompasses such top cultural sights as the Adler Planetarium, Shedd Aquarium and the Field Museum, with pedestrian walkways linking all three.

Top 25

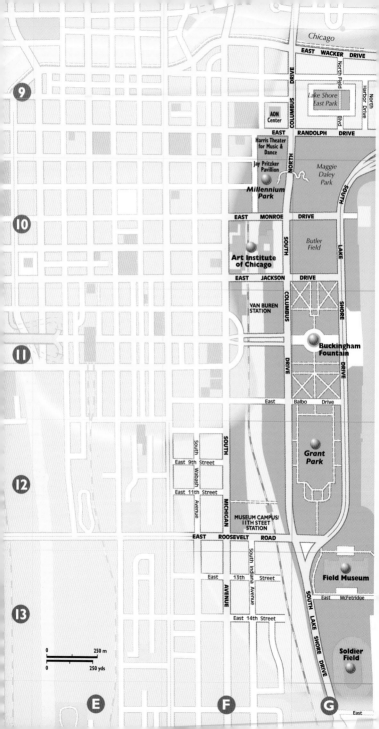

DuSable
Harbor

Lake

Michigan

Monroe
Harbor

Chicago
Harbor

Shedd
Aquarium

East   Solidarity   Drive

**Adler
Planetarium**

Drive

Burnham
Harbor

Northerly
Island

Huntington
Bank
Pavilion

South   Lynn   White   Drive

Special

Olympic

Drive

Waldron   Drive

H

J

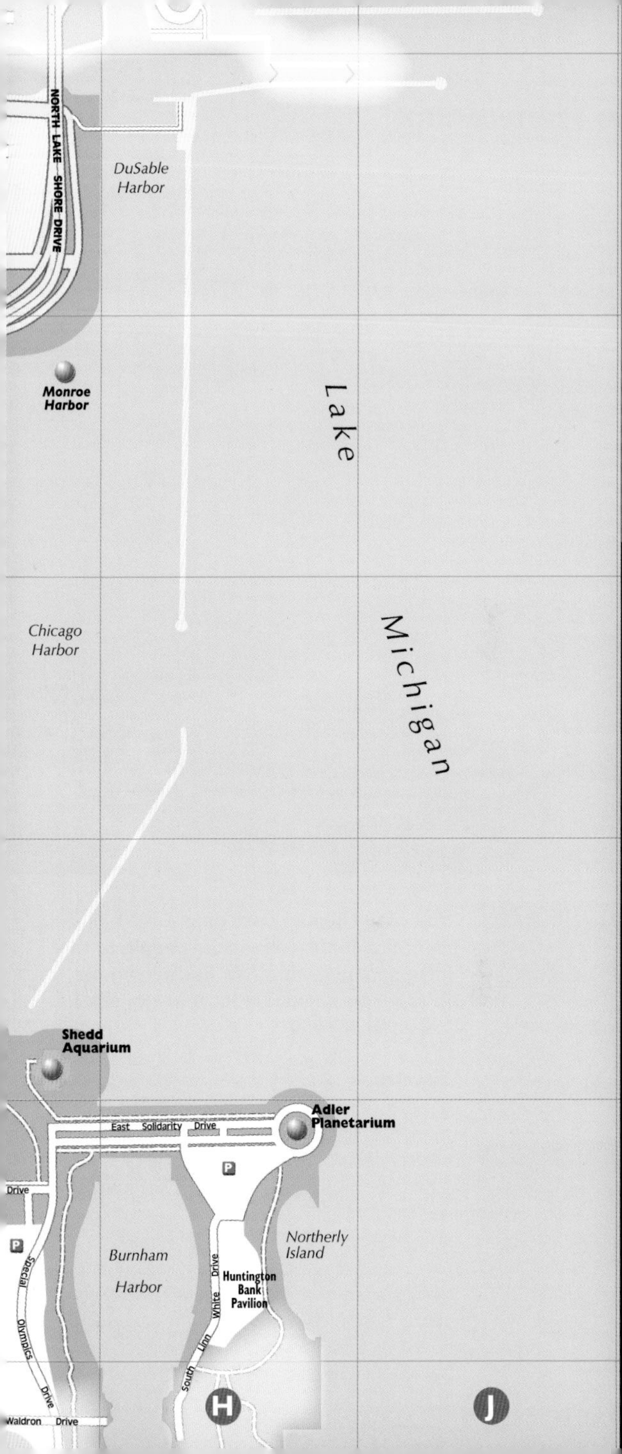

Adler Planetarium

HIGHLIGHTS

- Grainger Sky Theater
- Definiti Space Theater
- Doane Observatory
- Historic Atwood Sphere
- Space Visualization Laboratory

TIP

- Be prepared to pay for shows to experience the Adler in full.

Projecting the night sky onto a huge overhead dome, connecting people to the universe and each other, has helped the Adler Planetarium win local hearts since it opened in 1930.

Skywatching Max Adler, a Sears Roebuck executive, realized his ambition to put the wonders of the cosmos within the reach of ordinary people when he provided the money to have the western hemisphere's first modern planetarium built in Chicago.

The planetarium holds one of the world's major astronomical collections. This landmark building is a superb dodecahedron in rainbow granite, decorated with signs of the zodiac and topped by a lead-covered copper dome. The Grainger Sky Theater and Definiti Space Theater

Clockwise from left: The Adler Planetarium with the city in the background; the audience admires a planet in the Definiti Space Theater; the austere exterior of the Adler Planetarium belies the amazing sights within; a solar system exhibit

use digital technology and three-dimensional graphics to help you journey into space and through the stars.

Finding space Planet Explorers is a space exploration experience for kids. Other areas are devoted to how changing perceptions of the universe have affected human culture and the practicalities of exploring space, with items from manned exploration and samples of the Moon and Martian rock. Mission Moon lets visitors experience America's first steps into space through the eyes of NASA Captain James Lovell Jr. and his family.

The Adler's newest exhibition, Chicago's Night Sky, is an interactive experience for sharing stories of Chicago stargazers, past, present, professional as well as amateur.

THE BASICS

adlerplanetarium.org

✚ H13

✉ 1300 S. Lake Shore Drive

☎ 312/322-7827

🕐 Daily 9–4. Closed Thanksgiving, Dec 25. Hours are subject to change. Check website for closure/extension updates.

🍴 Café

🚇 Red, Green, Orange Lines: Roosevelt

🚌 146

♿ Good

💲 Moderate–Expensive

Art Institute of Chicago

Housed in a building erected together with the World's Columbian Exposition in 1893, the Art Institute has an acclaimed collection of Impressionist paintings. But its splendid galleries showcase a lot more, including the original trading room of the Stock Exchange.

Masterworks The celebrated *American Gothic* by Grant Wood and Edward Hopper's moody *Nighthawks* are among the highlights of the American collections. The Impressionist galleries and European art are on level 2, including a superb early Rembrandt and an amazing El Greco altarpiece. No work receives greater notice and admiration than Georges Seurat's expansive *A Sunday on La Grande Jatte*, a pointillist masterpiece. Seminal works

in adjacent galleries include *Haystacks* by Claude Monet, *Dancers* by Edgar Degas, a self-portrait on cardboard by Vincent van Gogh and the vibrant *Paris Street; Rainy Day* by Gustave Caillebotte. The Modern Wing houses 20th- and 21st-century art.

Curiosities Everything from Chinese ceramics to Guatemalan textiles has a niche on the first floor. Leave time for the stunning 1898 Trading Room of the Chicago Stock Exchange, designed by Louis Sullivan and reconstructed here. The lower level photography gallery exhibits works from its comprehensive collection and the Thorne Miniature Rooms re-create 68 historic settings in 1-inch-to-1-foot (2.5cm-to-30cm) scale. There are changing exhibitions from all over the world, and a well-curated shop.

THE BASICS

artic.edu

⊞ F10

✉ 111 S. Michigan Avenue

☎ 312/443-3600

🕐 Mon–Wed, Fri–Sun 10.30–5, Thu 10.30–8

🍴 Cafés

🚇 Brown, Orange Lines: Adams

🚌 3, 4, 6, 7, 126, 147, 151

♿ Good

💰 Expensive; free to Illinois residents Thu 5–8

❓ Free tours daily via app

Field Museum

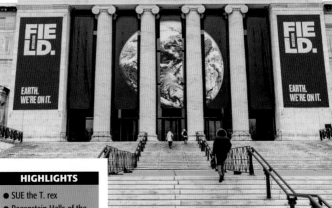

HIGHLIGHTS

- SUE the T. rex
- Regenstein Halls of the Pacific
- Dinosaur Hall
- Crown Family PlayLab
- Pawnee Earth Lodge
- The Ancient Americas
- 3-D movies
- Evolving Planet

TIPS

- This vast museum requires a visit plan, and the menu of options often includes blockbuster touring exhibitions.
- In fair weather, have a picnic on the front or back steps of the museum.

The Field displays wonderful exhibits from all corners of the globe. While here, ponder the fact that only around one percent of the museum's 40 million artifacts and specimens are on display.

The building The Field Museum's first home was originally established in 1894 in the Palace of Fine Arts in Jackson Park and housed a collection from the 1893 World's Columbian Exposition. As the museum's collection continued to grow, the search began for a site near Grant Park. By 1920, the current building was completed. The building's many sequestered galleries make an adventure of exploring the dinosaur galleries, the taxidermied World of Mammals, the life of an underground bug and corners of investigation.

Clockwise from left: Stone columns mark the entrance to the museum; Egyptian mummy masks; a magnificent sunstone; an Albertosaurus on display in the Stanley Field Hall

Great exhibits Upon entering the museum, Máximo the Titanosaur, the world's largest dinosaur ever discovered, takes pride of place in the main hall. Search out SUE the T. rex, the largest and most complete Tyrannosaurus rex specimen ever discovered, in an immersive gallery in the Griffin Halls of Evolving Planet to enjoy a unique multimedia experience. Other exhibits allow you to discover major ancient Egyptian artifacts arranged in and around a life-size, re-created tomb of a 5th-dynasty pharaoh. Another fascinating display is entitled "Traveling the Pacific," and is a powerful examination of cultural and spiritual life in Pacific cultures and the threats posed by the Western world's encroachment. Also note-worthy is the gem collection, which includes precious pieces by Tiffany & Co.

THE BASICS

fieldmuseum.org

➕ G13

✉ 1400 S. Lake Shore Drive

☎ 312/922-9410

🕐 Daily 9–5

🍴 The Field Bistro and Explorer Café

🚇 Red, Orange, and Green Lines: Roosevelt

🚌 Roosevelt Road

🚍 146

♿ Good

💵 Expensive

Shedd Aquarium TOP 25

MUSEUM CAMPUS TOP 25

HIGHLIGHTS

- Pacific white-sided dolphins
- Beluga whales
- Sea otters
- Sea anemones
- Penguins
- Turtles
- Sharks

Chicago's "Ocean-by-the-Lake" is the world's largest indoor aquarium, enhanced by an excellent state-of-the-art oceanarium where dolphins and whales show off natural behaviors, and a Philippine reef exhibit showcases sharks.

Aquarium A re-created Caribbean coral reef at the core of this imposing Greek-style building is the watery home to barracuda, moray eels, nurse sharks and many other creatures who are fed several times daily by a skilled team of microphone-equipped divers. While in the tank with the various marine life, the divers describe the creatures and inform about their habits and their habitat. Around the reef, denizens of the deep waters of the world occupy geographically arranged habitats.

48

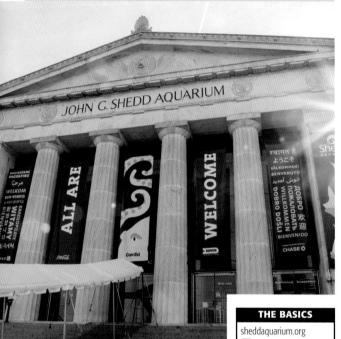

Clockwise from top left: Dolphins delight their onlookers; the handsome stone entrance; a turtle enjoys a swim; a curious gentoo penguin

Oceanarium Several times daily, learn about amazing animal adaptations in an aquatic presentation with a changing line-up of favorite animals—Pacific white-sided dolphins, beluga whales or birds of prey. Winding nature trails lead to the lower-level windows that provide an underwater view of the dolphins and whales. You also see a colony of penguins and sea otters. Descend by elevator to the Wild Reef to see fascinating tropical creatures such as sea dragons, whiptail rays and lionfish. Only a delicate, 0.25-inch- (0.6cm-) thick window separates visitors from 30 sharks swimming in a massive floor-to-ceiling tank, which re-creates a reef in the Philippines. Organized activities also go on in the evenings and the "Asleep with the Fishes" sleepovers are especially popular with children.

THE BASICS

sheddaquarium.org

⊞ G12

✉ 1200 S. Lake Shore Drive

☎ 312/939-2438

🕐 Jun–Aug daily 9–6; Sep–May Mon–Fri 9–5. Last entry 45 minutes before closing

🍴 Soundings Restaurant; Deep Ocean Café; snacks at Bubble Net Food Court

Ⓜ Red Line: Roosevelt

🚌 146

🍴 Excellent

💲 Expensive; free on Community Discount Days; some exhibits at reduced fee; Asleep with the Fishes expensive

Millennium Park

TOP 25

Jay Pritzker Pavilion (left) and Cloud Gate *by Anish Kapoor (right)*

THE BASICS

millenniumpark.org

⊞ F10

✉ 201 E. Randolph Drive

☎ 312/742-1168

🍴 Park Grill

Ⓜ Brown, Green, Orange, Pink Lines: Washington/Wabash

🚍 4, 60, 124, 151, 157

♿ Good

🎫 Free

HIGHLIGHTS

● Jay Pritzker Pavilion
● *Cloud Gate* (The Bean), Anish Kapoor
● Crown Fountain
● BP Bridge
● Maggie Daley Park
● Ice-skating rink
● Lurie Garden
● Boeing Galleries (contemporary art and sculptures)

This art- and architecture-filled park is Chicago's crown jewel. Take a selfie at "The Bean," the most popular city sculpture, then enjoy the gardens, water-play area and frequent concerts.

Cutting-edge culture City planner Daniel Burnham put his stamp on Grant Park in the early 1900s, giving the city an apron of green at its front door. Millennium Park updates the civic respite concept with new landmarks by design-world greats including architect Frank Gehry, who brought his signature swooping-titanium style to the erection of the park's central theater, the Jay Pritzker Pavilion. Gehry also designed the winding bridge (308yd/281m) that leads toward the lake. The Crown Fountain's twin glass towers (50ft/15m) project video images of a cross section of Chicagoans in portrait, while in summer children run beneath the water jets. The park also has plazas, gardens, promenades and a restaurant.

The Bean Briton Anish Kapoor created the 110-ton elliptical sculpture *Cloud Gate*, affectionately called "The Bean" by locals. Its highly polished surface bends and warps the surrounding skyline in reflection, a sight that attracts many photographers. The city tried to block people from capturing its image, claiming copyright infringement. Public uproar followed and officials relented, though the city maintains that anyone seeking to publish images of "The Bean" needs the permission of the artist.

More to See

BUCKINGHAM FOUNTAIN

Among the features of Grant Park is the 1926 Buckingham Fountain. Designed by Edward H. Bennett, it is notable for its choreographed colorful lights dancing on the 1.5 million gallons (6.8 million liters) of water that are pumped daily.

🔲 G11 ✉ Grant Park 🕐 Apr to mid-Oct 8am–11pm

GRANT PARK

Planned by Daniel Burnham in 1909 as the centerpiece of a series of lakefront parks, Grant Park is a major festival venue that has seen everything from a violence-marred 1968 anti-Vietnam War demonstration to a papal Mass in 1979. Grant Park is essentially a succession of lawns crisscrossed by walkways and split in two by busy Lake Shore Drive. Bordered by the high-rises of the Loop and the expanses of Lake Michigan, Grant Park never lets you forget that you are in Chicago. Its Petrillo Music Shell provides a setting for summer concerts.

🔲 G12 ✉ Bordered by S. Michigan Avenue, E. Randolph Drive, E. Roosevelt Road and Lake Michigan ☎ 312/742-3918 🕐 Visit during daylight hours only, except for special evening events 🚇 Brown, Orange Lines: State/Lake, Washington or Adams 🚌 3, 4, 6, 38, 60, 145, 146, 147, 151, 157

MONROE HARBOR

Some 1,000 boats moor at this harbor, just across Lake Shore Drive from Grant Park, providing a picturesque foreground for a lakefront stroll.

🔲 G10 ✉ Grant Park

SOLDIER FIELD

soldierfield.net

The original 1924 colonnaded Greek Revival stadium is home to football's Chicago Bears. A 2003 addition resembling a glass-and-steel spaceship set down within the classic arcade wall updated the services of the stadium.

🔲 G13 ✉ 1410 S. Museum Campus Drive ☎ 312/235-7000 🚇 Red, Orange, Green Lines: Roosevelt 🚌 146

Buckingham Fountain in Grant Park

A Walk in the Park

A stroll through Chicago's front yard takes you to and past some of the city's best cultural attractions and mostly away from car traffic.

DISTANCE: Around 2 miles (3km) **ALLOW:** 90 minutes without museum stops

START

SOLDIER FIELD (▷ 51) 🚩 G13
🚉 Red, Orange, Green Lines: Roosevelt

END

PARK GRILL (▷ 54) 🚩 F10
🚉 Brown, Orange, Green, Pink Lines: Washington/Wabash

1 Begin on the south end of Grant Park (▷ 51) at Soldier Field, where a classic, Greek-columned sports arena somewhat incongruously holds a massive spaceship-shape dish.

8 Stroll past the Gehry-designed stage, through the garden to Anish Kapoor's mirror-like *Cloud Gate*. End your trip with a park-view meal at the Park Grill.

2 Turn north to face the back of the Field Museum (▷ 46), which houses 40 million artifacts in its more than a century old collection.

7 Cross Monroe Drive and veer slightly east through Grant Park to pick up the start of the Frank Gehry-designed BP Bridge, which winds its way into Millennium Park (▷ 50).

3 Walk north around the Field Museum. The Adler Planetarium (▷ 42) will be lakeward to your right, as is the Shedd Aquarium (▷ 48), the world's largest such indoor attraction.

6 Walk north along Columbus Drive, passing the Petrillo Music Shell and the back side of the Art Institute of Chicago (▷ 44).

4 Follow the Museum Campus sidewalks past the entrance of the Shedd to the promenade that skirts Monroe Harbor (▷ 51). In summer the harbor is full of boats.

5 Continue north along Monroe Harbor, crossing Lake Shore Drive at a designated crossing, to Buckingham Fountain (▷ 51) to see the ornate landmark with its central jet.

Entertainment and Nightlife

CHICAGO SUMMER DANCE

cityofchicago.org

Thursday through Sunday afternoons throughout the summer, the city of Chicago hosts a free dance party in the Spirit of Music Garden in Grant Park, with live bands and dance lessons. Organizers set down a massive dance floor, where people are invited to dance to swing or salsa or whatever the night's music theme may be. All dance levels are welcome.

➕ G12 ✉ Grant Park (▷ 51)

CINDY'S

cindysrooftopbar

This popular rooftop nightspot is famous for its open-air terrace that overlooks both Millennium Park and Lake Michigan. Located in the architecturally stunning Chicago Athletic Association Hotel (▷ 112), advanced reservations are recommended. Prices are steep, but well worth it for the views, quality food and drink.

➕ F10 ✉ 12 S. Michigan Avenue
☎ 312/792-3502 🚇 Brown, Green, Red, Pink, Purple Lines: Washington/Wabash 🚌 3, 146, 147, 151, 157

HARRIS THEATER

harristheaterchicago.org

Popular Harris Theater hosts a 1,500-seat venue devoted primarily to performances of both local and visiting dance troupes.

➕ F9 ✉ 205 E. Randolph Drive ☎ 312/334-7777 🚇 Brown, Green, Orange Lines: Randolph 🚌 4, 60, 147, 151, 157

JAY PRITZKER PAVILION

grantparkmusicfestival.com

From June to August the Grant Park Music Festival holds free classical, jazz and pop concerts on Wednesday, Friday

GRANT PARK'S BLUES AND JAZZ

Each June and September the Petrillo Music Shell in Grant Park (▷ 51) is the stage for blues and jazz festivals respectively, which draw top international names as well as the city's greats in both fields. The performers are greeted by tens of thousands of fans, who arrive with blankets and picnic supplies to enjoy the free music.

and Saturday evenings. The Grant Park Orchestra and visiting guests play.

➕ F10 ✉ 201 E. Randolph Drive
☎ 312/742-1168 🚇 Brown, Green, Red, Pink, Purple Lines: Washington/Wabash 🚌 3, 146, 147, 151, 157

THE JOFFREY BALLET

joffrey.org

One of the world's premiere dance companies regularly performs classical ballets including Romeo & Juliet and The Nutcracker, as well as modern dance pieces.

➕ F9 ✉ 10 E. Randolph Street ☎ 312/386-8905 🚇 Red Line: State 🚌 2, 29, 146, 148

LOLLAPALOOZA

lollapalooza.com

One of the most popular music festivals in the US, this four-day summer festival draws dozens of big-name, A-list and buzzed-about rock, alternative, hip-hop and punk bands. Dance, comedy and crafts are a popular part of the festival, as is Kidzapalooza, an area which holds kids' rock concerts and different music activities. Buy tickets for Lollapalooza when they go on sale in spring, because they sell out fast.

➕ G12 ✉ Grant Park (▷ 51) 🚇 Green, Orange, Red Lines: Roosevelt ☎ 888/512-7469 (tickets) 🚌 3, 4, 6, 146

Where to Eat

PRICES
Prices are approximate, based on a 3-course meal for one person.
$$$$ over $50
$$$ $31–$50
$$ $16–$30
$ up to $15

BROWN BAG SEAFOOD CO. ($$)
brownbagseafood.com
Offering healthy, quick and affordable seafood overlooking Maggie Daley Park. Enjoy dining alfresco when the weather is clement.
➕ G9   ✉ 340 E. Randolph Street
☎ 312/496-3999   ⏱ Lunch and dinner daily   🚇 Brown, Orange, Green, Pink Lines: Washington/Wabash   🚌 4, 60

EGGY'S DINER ($$)
eggysdiner.com
Hidden within Lake Shore East, this diner featuring traditional breakfast and lunch offerings is popular with locals.
➕ F9   ✉ 333 E. Benton Place   ☎ 773/234-3449   ⏱ Breakfast and lunch daily   🚇 Brown, Orange, Green, Pink Lines: Washington/Wabash   🚌 4, 60

FIELD BISTRO ($$)
fieldmuseum.org
Field Bistro, within the Field Museum, features locally sourced food and a rotating selection of exclusive craft brews. The beers are inspired by the museum's collection.
➕ G13   ✉ 1400 S. Lake Shore Drive
☎ 312/922-9410   ⏱ Lunch daily   🚇 Green, Orange, Red Lines: Roosevelt   🚌 130, 146

PARK GRILL ($$$)
parkgrillchicago.com
Millennium Park's signature restaurant overlooks the skating rink in winter and uses the pavilion for outdoor dining in summer. Lunch options focus on hamburgers, pastas and salads. Dinner features American classics.
➕ F10   ✉ 11 N. Michigan Avenue
☎ 312/521-7275   ⏱ Lunch and dinner daily   🚇 Brown, Orange, Green, Pink Lines: Washington/Wabash   🚌 3, 20, 147, 151, 157

SOUNDINGS CAFÉ ($$)
sheddaquarium.org
Panoramic lake views wrap around the family-friendly casual café and coffee shop at the Shedd Aquarium. The menu features dishes made with organic, locally grown produce, including a range of salads and sandwiches.
➕ G12   ✉ 1200 S. Lake Shore Drive
☎ 312/692-3277   ⏱ Breakfast and lunch daily 🚇 Green, Orange, Red Lines: Roosevelt
🚌 130, 146

TERZO PIANO ($$$)
terzopianochicago.com
Located in the Modern Wing of the Art Institute of Chicago, lunch at this natural light-filled restaurant overlooking the city's skyline features delicious dishes made from scratch using organically grown produce and farm-raised meats and poultry.
➕ F10   ✉ 159 E. Monroe Street   ⏱ Lunch daily   ☎ 312/443-8650   🚇 Blue, Red Lines: Monroe; Brown, Orange, Pink, Green: Adams
🚌 3, 4, 6, 7, 147, 151

THE TASTE OF CHICAGO
Chicagoans love to eat and do so with gusto by the thousand at the annual Taste of Chicago festival in Grant Park. Usually held in July, around 100 local restaurants dispense their creations, often in affordable "taste-size" portions, from open-front stalls. Free entertainment keeps toes tapping.

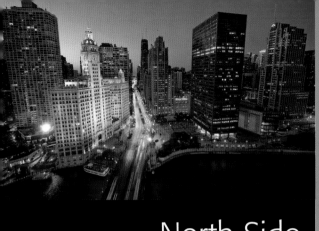

North Side

North of the Chicago River are parks buffering the lakeshore and the city's most chic shopping district, the Magnificent Mile, as well as the Gold Coast, one of Chicago's priciest residential districts.

Top 25

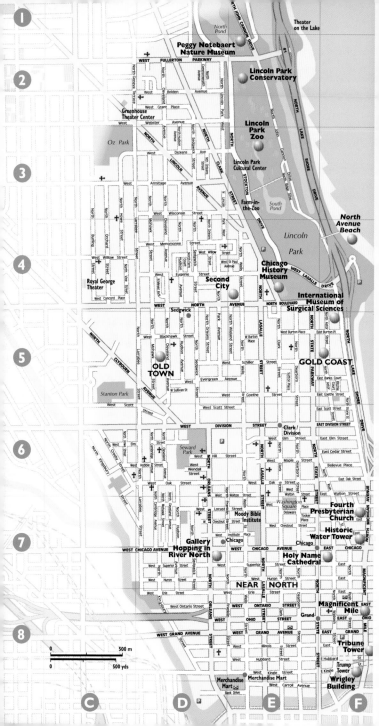

1

North Pond

North John Cannon Drive

Theater on the Lake

Peggy Notebaert Nature Museum

2

WEST FULLERTON PARKWAY

North Cleveland Avenue
North Geneva Terrace
West Belden Avenue
North Lincoln Avenue

West Grant Place
Greenhouse Theater Center
West Webster Avenue

Lincoln Park Conservatory

Lincoln Park Zoo

Oz Park

NORTH

West Dickens Avenue
North Halsted Street
North Mohawk Ave
North Orchard Street
North Cleveland
North Fremont

LINCOLN

CLARK STREET

AVENUE

N. Jones

Lincoln Park Cultural Center

Farm-in-the-Zoo

South Pond

North Avenue Beach

3

West Armitage Avenue

West Wisconsin Street
West Menomonee Street

North Howe Street
North Burling Street
North Orchard Street
North Vine Street
North Larrabee Street
North Mohawk
North Cleveland Avenue
North Sedgwick Street

North Park West
West St Paul Avenue
West Eugenie Street
West Concord Place

North Wells Street

DRIVE

Lincoln Park

WEST LASALLE DRIVE

4

Royal George Theater

Second City

West Willow Street
Court
Hudson
West St Paul Ave
N Mohawk St

NORTH AVENUE

Chicago History Museum

International Museum of Surgical Sciences

NORTH BOULEVARD

Sedgwick

WEST NORTH AVENUE

North LaSalle Street

North State Parkway

West Burton Place
East Burton Pl.

Clark Street

5

OLD TOWN

West Blackhawk Street
North Hudson Avenue
North Cleveland Ave
North Mohawk Street
North Orleans Avenue
North Wieland Street

West Schiller Street
West Evergreen Avenue
West Goethe Street

W Sullivan St

West Scott Street

West Goethe Street

Stanton Park

North Kingsbury

CLYBOURN

AVENUE

Sutton Place
Astor Street

LASALLE STREET

STATE PARKWAY

GOLD COAST

East Burton Place
East Banks Court
Stone Court
Scott Ct
East Goethe Street
North Stone St
North Dearborn Street

LAKE SHORE DRIVE

6

WEST DIVISION STREET

Seward Park

West Hill Street
West Wendall Street
West Oak Street
West Walton Street

North Cambridge Ave
North View Street
West Elm Street
North Hooker
West Hobbie Street
North Cleveland
North Larrabee
North Mohawk
North Hudson
North Orleans

ORLEANS STREET

NORTH LASALLE STREET

CLARK STREET

Washington Square

Clark/ Division

EAST DIVISION STREET

West Elm Street
East Elm Street
East Cedar Street
Bellevue Place
East Oak Street

7

Gallery Hopping in River North

Moody Bible Institute

West Locust Street
West Chestnut Street

Chicago

WEST CHICAGO AVENUE

West Superior Street
West Huron Street
West Erie Street

North Sedgwick

West Walton Street
West Locust Street
West Chestnut Street

Chicago

WEST CHICAGO AVENUE

Locust Place
Tooker Place
Delaware

Fourth Presbyterian Church

Historic Water Tower

Holy Name Cathedral

Chicago

EAST CHICAGO AVENUE

East Superior Street
East Huron Street
East Erie Street

Magnificent Mile

MAGNIFICENT MILE

NORTH MICHIGAN AVENUE

NEAR NORTH

North State Street

8

West Ontario Street
West Ohio Street

WEST GRAND AVENUE

West Hubbard Street
West Kinzie Street

Merchandise Mart

Bank Drive

ORLEANS STREET

North Dearborn Street

EAST ONTARIO STREET
East Ohio Street

EAST GRAND AVENUE

Grand

Merchandise Mart

West Carroll Avenue

North State Street

Tribune Tower

Trump Tower

Wrigley Building

East Hubbard
East Kinzie St

0   500 m
0   500 yds

C   D   E   F

Lake

Michigan

Oak Street
Beach

East Lake Shore Drive

**360
CHICAGO**
East Delaware Place

Chestnut   Seneca   North De Witt Plaza

Pearson   Street   Lake Shore Park
Seneca
Park
AVENUE   **Museum of
Contemporary Art**

Superior   Street

NORTH

Huron   Street

FAIRBANKS

Erie   Street

St. Clair

ONTARIO   **STREET**
McClurg

STREET
COURT

AVENUE

Illinois   St

**NBC
Tower**

North   Water   Street

**Centennial Fountain
& Arc**

Chicago

LAKE

North St

East   Grand

East   Illinois

DRIVE

Avenue

Street

DuSable
Park Site

Outer
Harbor

Milton Lee
Olive Park

Ohio Street
Beach

**Chicago
Children's
Museum**

**Centennial
Wheel**

NORTH STREETERIDR

Navy Pier

**Aon Grand
Ballroom**

G   **H**   **J**

360 CHICAGO

HIGHLIGHTS

- 80-mile (129km) visibility
- Views of the skyline at night
- Lean out over the top of the building in a clear-glass box, on the thrill-seeking experience TILT
- BAR 94 for snacks and libations
- Bonus activities daily

Ride the elevator to 360 CHICAGO on the 94th floor of the city's iconic skyscraper, 875 N. Michigan Avenue, formerly called the John Hancock Center, for expansive views by day or by night.

The observatory There are far-reaching vistas in every direction at 360 CHICAGO where, on a clear day, visitors can see for 80 miles (129km) and four surrounding states. An entertaining multimedia tour, included in the admission price, highlights the skyscrapers and Chicago history. For an extra fee, thrill-seekers can try the innovative TILT, which literally tilts people over the edge of the skyscraper in a glass box, so they face down to the street 1,000ft (305m) below. Grab a gelato, craft cocktail or local brew at BAR 94 and watch the sun set

Clockwise from top left: Visitors enjoy far-reaching views; the spectacular city view and beyond, looking down from 360 CHICAGO; the TILT is not for the fainthearted

and lights come up. Daily bonus activities are available with general admission, plus paid additions including weekend yoga. Special packages such as the Sun and Stars package allow a second admission after dark to allow you to admire the city's nighttime skyline in all its twinkling glory.

The building Solid at its base and tapering as it goes skyward, 875 N. Michigan Avenue, designed by the renowned firm Skidmore, Owings & Merrill, is divided nearly equally between residential and commercial use and, at 1,500ft (457.2m), is the fourth-highest building in Chicago. It was constructed using a revolutionary external strengthening system, getting away from traditional internal pillars and thus creating more usable space on each floor.

THE BASICS

360chicago.com

⊞ F7

✉ 875 N. Michigan Avenue

☎ 360 Chicago: 888/875-8439

🕒 Daily 9am–11pm

🍴 BAR 94 (at 360 Chicago)

🚇 Red Line: Chicago

🚌 143, 145, 146, 147, 151

♿ Some

💲 360 CHICAGO: Expensive

Gallery Hopping in River North

HIGHLIGHTS

- Addington Gallery
- Carl Hammer Gallery
- Weinberg/Newton Gallery
- Byron Roche Gallery
- Zolla/Lieberman Gallery
- Maya Polsky Gallery

Dozens of art dealers occupy the former warehouses in River North's most handsome district for one-stop art shopping. Tours of galleries happen on Saturday.

From industry to art Chicago's gallery district claims roughly 70 art sellers in the heart of River North, bounded by Chicago Avenue on the north, the Chicago River on the south, LaSalle to the east and Orleans to the west. The area boomed with industry, beginning in the 1890s when railroad tracks lined the north bank of the Chicago River, earning it the nickname "Smokey Hollow." River North slid slowly into decay as factories gradually closed in the 1950s and '60s. In the 1970s, attracted by low rents and large spaces, artists began to move in. Later, galleries followed, cementing the art

scene in the district of redbrick warehouse buildings. Chain restaurants and condos have more recently driven up rents, but the galleries clustered on Huron and Superior streets have managed to survive the real-estate rush. The River North Design District contains showrooms filled with one-of-a-kind home decor items.

Art scene The most established artists showing in Chicago exhibit here alongside national and international names. Maya Polsky Gallery shows works by the late Ed Paschke. Addington Gallery shows paintings made with hot wax and Carl Hammer Gallery displays works from Outsider artists including Joseph Yoakum. All are open to the public but to visit with a guide, be at 714 N. Street at 11am any Saturday, where the free tours kick off.

THE BASICS

⊕ D7

✉ Between the Chicago River and Chicago Avenue, LaSalle and Orleans streets

🕐 Gallery hours vary; most open Tue–Sat 10–6

🍽 Restaurants, cafés and coffee shops nearby

🚇 Brown Line: Chicago

🚌 37, 66

♿ Good

✋ Free

Lincoln Park Zoo

HIGHLIGHTS

● Regenstein African Journey
● Regenstein Center for African Apes
● Kovler Seal Pool
● Robert and Mayari Pritzker Penguin Cove
● Pritzker Family Children's Zoo
● Regenstein Macaque Forest
● Regenstein Small Mammal-Reptile House

TIP

● The sea lions are fed daily at 10:30am and 2pm.

Free to the public and a city block from a popular residential district, the zoo is a local favorite, with nearly 200 species to see and learn about.

Small beginnings Created out of sand dunes, swamp and the former city cemetery, Lincoln Park was established by the 1870s after its zoo had been started with the gift of two pairs of swans from New York's Central Park. Evolving over 150 years through the contributions of various designers, it is one of the most-established zoos and the only privately managed free-admission zoo in the country.

Wild kingdom The zoo, a block east of Lincoln Park, is very much a part of city life, where passersby can drop in on a troop of gorillas or

Clockwise from left: A polar bear cooling off; an elegant giraffe; Lincoln Park Zoo entrance; tigers grooming each other; the zoo is colorfully lit up at night; the gorilla enclosure

the swimming polar bears. Early 20th-century brick buildings house birds, mammals and some primates, but a spate of new building has brought more immersive exhibits to the zoo. Regenstein African Journey creates an atmospheric passage through habitats for pygmy hippos, deerlike klipspringers, wild dogs, towering giraffes and even cockroaches. Regenstein Center for African Apes lets the light shine into vine-covered and bamboo-planted indoor living areas, supplemented by outdoor grounds. The Children's Zoo combines a climbing area and interactive exhibits.

Down on the farm Farm-in-the-Zoo's white-trimmed red barn is an unusual building, full of activities for young learners, and emphasizes interactive nature play.

THE BASICS

lpzoo.org

✚ E3

✉ 2001 N. Clark Street

☎ 312/742-2000

🕐 Jun–Aug Mon–Fri 10–5, Sat–Sun 10–6.30; Apr–May, Sep–Oct daily 10–5; Nov–Mar 10–4.30

🍴 Restaurant and cafés

Ⓜ Brown, Purple Lines: Armitage; Brown, Red Lines: Fullerton

🚌 22, 36, 151, 156

♿ Good

💵 Free

Navy Pier

HIGHLIGHTS

- Centennial Ferris Wheel
- Chicago Children's Museum
- Chicago Shakespeare Theater and The Yard
- Boat rides
- AMC Navy Pier IMAX® Theatre
- City views from the Pier
- Offshore (the world's largest rooftop bar)

TIP

- The popular beer garden at the end of the Pier serves draft beer, snacks and a line-up of local bands in summer, with great skyline views.

One of the region's most popular destinations, Navy Pier is an evolving mix of culture, cuisine, entertainment and retail. A redesigned entrance plaza with a fountain greets visitors, who can stroll the pier snapping photos of the gorgeous skyline and Lake Michigan.

History and cruises Opened in 1916, Navy Pier was part of architect Daniel Burnham's vision for a new Chicago and combined shipping with dining and entertainment. The former steadily disappeared and the pier declined until a 1990s makeover saw it re-emerge as a stylish family-aimed entertainment venue in the heart of the city. The pier has encouraged a revival of water activity with a plethora of pleasure cruises departing from its edge along the South Dock.

Clockwise from left: Navy Pier Centennial Ferris Wheel; fountain outside the Children's Museum; the city provides a dramatic backdrop to Navy Pier

Entertainment Enclosed gondolas make it possible to ride the 196ft- (60m) high Centennial Ferris Wheel year-round. Crowds also come for the boat rides, Children's Museum, IMAX movies, a dancing water fountain for children to splash around in, motorized swings that spin 14ft (4m) off the floor, and more. On summer nights, sit in the beer garden and listen to live music while watching the fireworks shows.

Culture Take in a concert at one of Navy Pier's several stages. For intellectual balance, get tickets to the acclaimed Chicago Shakespeare Theater (▷ 76), modeled on the venues of the Bard's own day with seating surrounding the stage on three levels. The Chicago Children's Museum educates as it entertains (▷ 69).

THE BASICS

navypier.com
✚ H8
✉ 600 E. Grand Avenue
☎ 312/595-7437
🕐 Sun–Thu 10–8, Fri–Sat 10–10; Memorial Day–Labor Day Sun–Thu 10–10, Fri–Sat 10am–midnight
🍽 Various restaurants and cafés
🚇 Red Line: Grand
🚌 2, 29, 65, 66, 124
♿ Good
✋ Free; fee for individual attractions

North Avenue Beach

TOP 25

Outdoor activities at North Avenue Beach

THE BASICS

chicagoparkdistrict.com

➕ F4

✉ 1603 N. Lake Shore Drive

☎ 312/742-3224

🚇 Red Line: Clark/ Division

🚌 72

♿ Fair

✋ Free

HIGHLIGHTS

- Beach volleyball
- Chess Pavilion
- Ocean-liner bathhouse
- Upper-deck Castaways Bar & Grill
- Seasonal outdoor gym
- Swimming

Daily in summer, and especially on weekends and holidays, Chicagoans storm this beach, one of the liveliest and best equipped of the city's 25 beaches on the 26-mile (42km) Lake Michigan shore.

Games for all To mingle with Chicagoans, head to North Avenue Beach, a community playground for families, young singles, exercise fanatics and people watchers. The park is known as a volleyballer's delight, lined with net uprights used by teams as well as casual pick-up players (rent volleyball courts and equipment in advance). Rent a kayak and enjoy the skyline and do some sightseeing from the lake. Or you can head to the Chess Pavilion on the concrete biking and walking path south of the beach. Yoga classes are held both on the sand, and balancing on paddleboards in the lake. While you can watch Chicago's annual August Air and Water Show from beaches up and down the shore, the main action takes place at North Avenue, drawing many of the million people a day who view the displays.

Bathhouse The ocean-liner-looking building beached on the shore replaced the original landmark Depression-era bathhouse of the same design. The 2000 version has showers, restrooms and concession stands as well as beach chair, bike and volleyball equipment rentals. At the end of the day, try Castaways Bar & Grill for margaritas and beer, though it also serves salads and sandwiches.

Second City

Detail of the building's exterior (left); outside the theater (right)

From the stage at Second City, Chicago performers, some famous, popularized a form of improvised comedy now enjoyed on television and in cities around the world.

Their laurels The first name in improvisation, The Second City nurtured and popularized Chicago's brand of bold, quick wit and impactful sketch comedy. Since opening in 1959, the Old Town comedy theater has been shepherding talent including John Belushi, Bill Murray, Tina Fey, Keegan-Michael Key, Steve Carell and Stephen Colbert, and trains thousands of comedy students a year. With live comedy shows seven nights a week, Second City entertains locals and tourists alike with its signature two-act performances of written and improvised material tackling current events, pop culture and the nation's economic climate. Housed in the Piper's Alley building, it is home to three on-site dining options.

Improv comedy Improvisational comedy relies on actors supplying dialogue and action without the aid of a script. Developed as an art form by Viola Spolin in the 1930s, the methods were adopted by a group of University of Chicago students in the 1940s and '50s, who formed the Compass Players, a group that would later evolve into The Second City. To this day, improv is used by Second City performers to create and develop new material for their original comedy shows.

THE BASICS

secondcity.com
+ E4
✉ 1616 N. Wells Street
☎ 312/337-3992
🎭 Performances nightly
Ⓜ Brown Line: Sedgwick; Red Line: Clark
🚌 72, 156
♿ Fair
✋ Expensive

HIGHLIGHTS

- Four studio theaters
- Cabaret seating
- Central Old Town location near restaurants and bars
- Three resident stages: Mainstage, e.t.c., and UP Comedy Club

Shopping the Magnificent Mile

Wrigley Building; Tiffany's (center); shoppers throng the sidewalk (right)

THE BASICS

themagnificentmile.com

⊞ F8

✉ Michigan Avenue north of the Chicago River to its terminus at Oak Street

☎ 312/642-3570 (events)

Ⓠ Red Line: Chicago, Grand

🚌 3, 146, 151, 157

♿ Good

HIGHLIGHTS

● Water Tower and Pumping Station
● Bloomingdale's
● Nordstrom
● Saks Fifth Avenue
● American Girl Place

From the Chicago River to Oak Street Beach, this portion of Michigan Avenue known as Chicago's Magnificent Mile lines up designer boutiques and major department stores in one bustling stretch.

Shop till you drop Over 460 stores pack the mile, selling everything from designer goods by Louis Vuitton, precious jewelry at Cartier and the luxury menswear by Italian designer Ermenegildo Zegna to affordable fashions from Japanese brand UNIQLO. Between high and low ends are the major American department stores, including Nordstrom, known for its clothes and shoe selection; Neiman Marcus, famed for its designer racks; and city favorite Bloomingdale's, with its on-trend looks. Vertical malls such as 900 North Michigan, The Shops at North Bridge and Water Tower Place, provide a home for a number of name-brand retailers and independent boutiques. Doll collectors flock to American Girl Place, a doll store with a range of accessories.

Culture breaks Architectural icons line the street; the Wrigley Building (▷ 72) and the Tribune Tower (▷ 72) face each other on the south end of the street. Farther north, the Historic Water Tower (▷ 70) and Pumping Station, two of the few to survive the Great Fire of 1871, symbolize the city's rebirth on the thoroughfare. A block from Michigan Avenue, the Museum of Contemporary Art (▷ 71) shows cutting-edge work.

CHICAGO CHILDREN'S MUSEUM

chicagochildrensmuseum.org

More than 15 interactive exhibits and daily programming keep children ages 0–10 engaged and excited to explore. Firm favorites range from the Tinkering Lab, where children use real tools to create things, and Sound Lab, where they can create short movies, to Cloud Buster, a 37ft- (11m) tall climbable sculpture made of structural steel and a variety of materials, including wood, woven rope, fiberglass and artificial turf.
🔲 H8 ✉ Navy Pier, 700 E. Grand Avenue ☎ 312/527-1000 🕐 Daily 10–5 (till 8 on Thu) 🚇 Red Line: Grand 🚌 2, 29, 65, 66, 124 ♿ Good 💰 Moderate

CHICAGO HISTORY MUSEUM

chicagohistory.org

Spread throughout a Georgian-style brick building constructed in 1932, with a modern, glass-walled extension, every major facet in Chicago's rise from swampland to modern metropolis is discussed and illustrated in chronologically arranged galleries. Alongside changing temporary shows, there are outstanding permanent exhibits including Chicago: Crossroads of America and Lincoln's Chicago. The museum also has an extensive costume and textile collection including articles from world-renowned fashion designers as well as household textiles by Chicago-based artists such as Angelo Testa.
🔲 E4 ✉ 1601 N. Clark Street ☎ 312/642-4600 🕐 Mon, Wed–Sat 9.30–4.30, Tue 9.30am–9pm 🚇 Brown Line: Sedgwick 🚌 22, 36, 72, 151, 156 ♿ Good 💰 Moderate; free Tue (2–9pm)

FOURTH PRESBYTERIAN CHURCH

fourthchurch.org

This Gothic Revival church (1914) serves a congregation of Chicago's elite. It was the creation of American architect Ralph Adams Cram. Occasional but enjoyable lunchtime concerts pack the pews.

Chicago Children's Museum

🚩 F7 ✉ 126 E. Chestnut Street
☎ 312/787-4570 🕐 Mon–Fri 7.30am–9pm,
Sat 7.30–6, Sun 7.30–6.30 🚇 Red Line:
Chicago 🚌 146, 147, 151 ♿ Good

GOLD COAST
In the late 19th century, Chicago businessman Potter Palmer astonished his peers by erecting a mansion home on undeveloped land north of the Loop, close to Lake Michigan. As others followed, the area became known as the Gold Coast, its streets lined by the elegant homes of the well-to-do.
🚩 F5

HISTORIC WATER TOWER
This pseudo-Gothic construction, built by William Boyington in 1869, is one of Chicago's enduring landmarks and is the oldest building on the north side of the Chicago River.
🚩 F7 ✉ 806 N. Michigan Avenue
📷 First-floor photography gallery: 312/742-0808 🕐 Mon–Fri 10–7, Sat–Sun 10–5.
Closed holidays 🚇 Red Line: Chicago
🚌 3, 66, 146, 147, 151 ♿ Few 🎟 Free

HOLY NAME CATHEDRAL
holynamecathedral.org
This is the seat of the Catholic Archdiocese of Chicago (1878). Built after the Great Chicago Fire of 1871, its cornerstone was laid in 1874. The cathedral features a towering Gothic Revival design.
🚩 F7 ✉ 730 N. Wabash Avenue
☎ 312/787-8040 🚇 Red Line: Chicago
🚌 36, 66 ♿ Good ❓ Check website for tours

INTERNATIONAL MUSEUM OF SURGICAL SCIENCES
imss.org
While many are drawn to this museum for its surgical instruments and apothecary artifacts, its four floors are filled with paintings as well as illustrations and sculptures that give an insight into pre-modern and modern healing practices.
🚩 F5 ✉ 1524 N. Lake Shore Drive
☎ 312/642-6502 🕐 Mon–Fri 9.30–5, Sat–Sun 10–5 🚇 Brown Line: Sedgwick
🚌 151 ♿ Good 🎟 Moderate ❓ Guided tour Thu 2pm

The Hall of Mortals at the International Museum of Surgical Sciences

Historic Water Tower

LINCOLN PARK CONSERVATORY

lincolnparkconservancy.org

The Conservatory (1891) has four separate greenhouses: the Orchid House, Fern Room, Show House and Palm House. Each one contains dazzling tropical and subtropical blooms as well as seasonal displays. Beyond the greenhouses there are magnificent gardens in different styles, a fountain and a Shakespeare monument.

⊞ E2 ⊠ 2391 N. Stockton Drive ☎ Conservatory: 312/742-7736 ⏰ Daily 9–5 🚇 Brown, Red Lines: Armitage 🚌 22, 36, 151, 156 ♿ Good 💵 Free

MUSEUM OF CONTEMPORARY ART

mcachicago.org

Items from the permanent collection of more than 2,500 artworks appear regularly in the museum's rotating exhibitions. The lower levels house temporary exhibitions and provide access to the Sculpture Garden. Free guided tours are available. Marisol, the on-site restaurant, serves seasonal cuisine in an interior designed by artist Chris Ofili.

⊞ F7 ⊠ 220 E. Chicago Avenue ☎ 312/280-2660 ⏰ Tue, Fri 10–9, Wed–Thu, Sat–Sun 10–5 🍴 Restaurant and bar 🚇 Red Line: Chicago 🚌 66, 157 ♿ Good 💵 Moderate ❓ Guided tours daily (45 min)

OAK STREET BEACH

The closeness of the exclusive Gold Coast neighborhood helps make Oak Street Beach the gathering place for some of Chicago's richest and best-toned bodies. See the huge mural at the Oak Street Beach underpass access.

⊞ F6 ⊠ Access from junction of N. Michigan Avenue and E. Lake Shore Drive 🚌 146, 147, 151

OLD TOWN

oldtownchicago.org

Gentrified in the 1960s and '70s by artists, the Old Town area combines busy, restaurant-lined commercial

Beautiful floral displays surround the Conservatory in Lincoln Park

throughways and intimate leafy residential streets. The annual June art fair is a big draw.

➕ D5 ✉ Streets fan out from intersection of North Avenue and Wells Street 🚇 Brown Line: Sedgwick 🚌 9, 72, 156

THE PEGGY NOTEBAERT NATURE MUSEUM

naturemuseum.org

Lively exhibits explore the natural history of the Midwest, including a greenhouse Butterfly Haven, and information on the insect population of every household.

➕ E2 ✉ 2430 N. Cannon Drive ☎ 773/755-5100 🕐 Mon–Fri 9–5, Sat–Sun 10–5 🚇 Brown, Red Lines: Fullerton 🚌 22, 36, 151, 156 ♿ Good 💲 Moderate; donations

THE TRIBUNE TOWER

In the 1920s, the *Chicago Tribune* staged a competition to decide the design of its new premises. The resulting neo-Gothic building is best admired from the exterior, inlaid with 120 stones from sites around the world including Greece's Parthenon and India's Taj Mahal. The former newsroom of the *Chicago Tribune* and the rest of the building have been converted into luxury condos since the building was sold in 2016.

➕ F8 ✉ 435 N. Michigan Avenue ☎ 312/222-3994 🚇 Red Line: Grand 🚌 3, 29, 65, 147, 151, 157 ♿ Good

THE WRIGLEY BUILDING

thewrigleybuilding.com

Partly modeled on the Giralda Tower in Seville, Spain, with ornamental features echoing the French Renaissance, the North and South structures are behind a facade linked by an arcaded walkway at street level and by two enclosed aerial walkways. The ornate glazed terra-cotta facade has retained its original gleam. The building is illuminated at night.

➕ F8 ✉ 400 N. Michigan Avenue ☎ 312/923-8080 🕐 Business hours 🚇 Red Line: Grand 🚌 3, 29, 65, 147, 151, 157 ♿ Good 💲 Free

The Wrigley Building

The ornate entrance to the Tribune Tower

One Magnificent Walk

Take in several architectural icons as well as the glitziest shopping in a mile-long walk up Michigan Avenue from the Chicago River.

DISTANCE: 1 mile (1.6 km) **ALLOW:** 2–3 hours

START

MICHIGAN AVENUE BRIDGE ⊞ F8
🚇 Red Line: Grand 🚌 3, 6, 29, 146, 151, 157

❶ Walk north across the Chicago River on Michigan Avenue Bridge, which in 1920 facilitated the rise of the so-called Magnificent Mile (▷ 68). Check out the Apple store (▷ 74).

❷ Two of the first structures erected after the bridge was built were the Wrigley Building (1921–24), to the left, and the Tribune Tower (1925), to the right (▷ 72).

❸ Farther north, opulent shops and hotels line Michigan Avenue. Fuel some heavy-duty window shopping with a bag of cheese popcorn from Garrett Popcorn, 625 N. Michigan at the corner with Ontario.

❹ One of the liveliest stores is Nike Town between Erie and Huron streets. Farther north is the Disney Store.

END

875 N. MICHIGAN AVENUE (▷ 58) ⊞ F7 🚇 Red Line: Chicago
🚌 146, 147, 151

❽ Finish the walk at 875 N. Michigan Avenue (1970), where 360 Chicago affords stunning views.

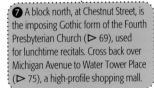

❼ A block north, at Chestnut Street, is the imposing Gothic form of the Fourth Presbyterian Church (▷ 69), used for lunchtime recitals. Cross back over Michigan Avenue to Water Tower Place (▷ 75), a high-profile shopping mall.

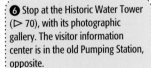

❻ Stop at the Historic Water Tower (▷ 70), with its photographic gallery. The visitor information center is in the old Pumping Station, opposite.

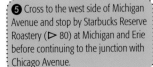

❺ Cross to the west side of Michigan Avenue and stop by Starbucks Reserve Roastery (▷ 80) at Michigan and Erie before continuing to the junction with Chicago Avenue.

NORTH SIDE WALK

Shopping

900 NORTH MICHIGAN SHOPS
shop900.com

This gleaming marble high-rise takes up a whole city block. Restaurants, cinemas and many stores are grouped around seven levels; a branch of Bloomingdale's is an anchor. The vast building is also home to more than 70 luxe retailers as well as smaller, exclusive boutiques.

⊞ F7 ✉ 900 N. Michigan Avenue
☎ 312/915-3916 🚇 Red Line: Chicago
🚌 146, 147, 151

AMERICAN GIRL PLACE
americangirl.com

At this doll store in Water Tower Place, you can not only buy a doll that looks like you but also get her hair styled, take her to tea and have your photo taken for the cover of a souvenir magazine.

⊞ F7 ✉ 835 N. Michigan Avenue
☎ 877/247-5223 🚇 Red Line: Chicago
🚌 3, 125, 143, 146, 147, 148, 151

APPLE
apple.com/retail/michiganavenue/

It's hard to miss Apple's Chicago downtown megastore, with its airy glass box, slinky curved-edge roof and glistening riverfront location. Stunning architecture

RANDOLPH STREET MARKET

Hundreds of vendors pack the old Beaux Arts Plumbers Hall at 1340 W. Randolph Street one weekend each month to sell a treasure trove of fun and funky items, like vintage brooches, retro decor and gourmet desserts. Local artists and entrepreneurs also launch new products here. Live entertainment and local craft beers add to the liveliness. An admission fee is charged at the gate, but pay in advance online (randolphstreetmarket.com) and you'll save a few bucks.

aside, it's also the site where Jean Baptiste Point du Sable, the city's first permanent settler, lived. Visitors check out Apple's latest tech gadgets and arrange meet-ups at the cascading staircases.

⊞ F8 ✉ 401 N. Michigan Avenue
☎ 312/529-9500 🚇 Brown, Orange, Green, Pink Lines: State/Lake; Red Line: Lake 🚌 3, 66, 146, 147, 151, 157

AZEEZA
azeeza.us

Local designer Azeeza Khan is known for her upscale and glam women's apparel and accessories. Her flagship boutique is located within the 900 Shops complex.

⊞ F7 ✉ 900 N. Michigan Avenue
☎ 312/649-9373 🚇 Red Line: Chicago
🚌 146, 147, 151

ELEMENTS
elementschicago.com

From home and outdoors decor to handbags, jewelry and fashion accessories, this treasure house of style and design features beautiful objects from around the world.

⊞ E7 ✉ 706 N. Wells Street ☎ 312/642-6574
🚇 Brown, Purple Lines: Chicago 🚌 37

IKRAM
ikram.com

Visitors can't miss this classy women's apparel boutique with its glossy lipstick-red exterior. Inside there's an art gallery and a café.

⊞ F7 ✉ 15 E. Huron Street ☎ 312/751-2739 🚇 Red Line: Chicago 🚌 36

KOKOROKOKO
kokorokokovintage.com

Miss the 1980s and '90s? This funky Wicker Park vintage shop sells

everything from cartoon buttons and stickers to vintage overalls and T-shirts. Nothing costs more than $100.

🔲 Off map ✉ 1323 N. Milwaukee Avenue
☎ 773/252-6996 🚇 Blue Line: Division
🚌 56

LEGO STORE

lego.com

LEGO fans can choose specific bricks in the "Pick-A-Brick Wall" while the "Living Room" lets kids build in-store.

🔲 F7 ✉ 835 N. Michigan Avenue
☎ 312/202-0946 🚇 Red Line: Chicago
🚌 146, 147, 151

NAVY PIER

navypier.com

Around 27 shops are gathered in this complex of restaurants and entertainment venues (▷ 64). This is a good place if you want souvenirs as gifts.

🔲 H8 ✉ 600 E. Grand Avenue ☎ 800/595-7437 🚇 Red Line: Grand 🚌 29, 65, 66, 129

P.O.S.H.

poshchicago.com

The expression "port out/starboard home," used by aristocrats seeking the shady side of the ship journeying between Britain and India, lends its name to this antiques shop specializing in vintage tabletop items from the early 19th century.

🔲 F8 ✉ 613 N. State Street ☎ 312/280-1602 🚇 Red Line: Grand 🚌 36, 65, 125

SEMICOLON

semicolonchi.com

The wonderful vision of one woman, D. L. Mullen, Semicolon is a beautiful mix of bookstore, community space and gallery—and is a BYOB as well.

🔲 C8 ✉ 515 N. Halsted Street ☎ 312/877-5170 🚇 Blue Line: Grand 🚌 8, 56, 65

MAGNIFICENT MILE

Michigan Avenue, home to many top-class and designer stores, is known as the "Magnificent Mile," a 1940s concept that eventually mutated into today's rows of marble-clad towers, mostly built during the 1970s and 1980s.

SHOPS AT THE MART

themart.com

Most of the vast Merchandise Mart is closed to the public, except for the first floor which features LuxeHome, 45 high-end kitchen and bath showrooms. The iconic city building is a design showpiece in itself, heralding from the art deco era of the 1930s.

🔲 E9 ✉ 350 N. Wells Street ☎ 800/677-6278 🚇 Brown, Purple Lines: Merchandise Mart 🚌 37, 125, 156

VOLUMES BOOKS

volumesbooks.com

A wonderfully curated and inviting indie bookshop, Volumes is conveniently located near Aster Hall food vaults on the 5th floor.

🔲 F7 ✉ 900 N. Michigan Avenue
☎ 312/846-6750 🚇 Red Line: Chicago
🚌 146, 147, 151

WATER TOWER PLACE

shopwatertower.com

Packing an incredible seven floors are a diverse range of clothing stores for men, women and children as well as a choice of jewelers, art galleries, home-furnishing emporiums, cinemas and restaurants. Specialty retailers include Accent Chicago and the Water Tower Clock and Watch Shop.

🔲 F7 ✉ 835 N. Michigan Avenue
☎ 312/440-3580 🚇 Red Line: Chicago
🚌 146, 147, 151

Entertainment and Nightlife

ANDY'S JAZZ CLUB
andysjazzclub.com
This popular club has some of the best live jazz in the city and has been going since the 1970s. Doors open at 4pm, and dinner is served daily from 4.30pm. Table reservations for dining only.
🔲 F8 ✉ 11 E. Hubbard Street ☎ 312/642-6805 🚇 Red Line: Grand 🚌 22, 36

THE BEAUTY BAR
thebeautybar.com
Manicures are given and martinis are served in the front of the bar until midnight. Meanwhile, in the back, the bar turns into a college-like dance party with retro tunes by artists including Madonna as well as '90s hits. Trivia nights, karaoke and other nightly events add to the fun.
🔲 A7 ✉ 1444 W. Chicago Avenue ☎ 312/226-8828 🚇 Blue Line: Chicago 🚌 9, 66

BILLY GOAT TAVERN
billygoattavern.com
This below-street-level, unpretentious watering hole and cheeseburger joint is a favorite among local journalists. It's noted as the inspiration for a famous television comedy sketch.
🔲 F8 ✉ 430 N. Michigan Avenue Lower Level (also at Navy Pier and other locations) ☎ 312/222-1525 🚇 Red Line: Grand 🚌 29, 65, 120, 121

NIGHTCLUB NEWS
The most general source is the Friday edition of the *Chicago Tribune* and its Metromix website (metromix.com). Inside info on the latest clubs, as well as the nightlife scene in general, can be found in the pages of the weekly *Chicago Reader* and on the websites for *New City* and *Time Out Chicago* magazines.

BLUE CHICAGO
bluechicago.com
This comfortable, homey blues club has been showcasing home-grown musical talent for more than 30 years.
🔲 E7 ✉ 536 N. Clark Street ☎ 312/661-0100 🚇 Red Line: Grand 🚌 22, 65
♿ Good

CHICAGO B.L.U.E.S. BAR
chicagobluesbar.com
One of the best little blues clubs in Chicago. On Sunday nights your admission here will also get you into Kingston Mines (▷ 77).
🔲 C3 ✉ 2519 N. Halsted Street ☎ 773/528-1012 🚇 Red, Brown Lines: Fullerton 🚌 8

CHICAGO SHAKESPEARE THEATER
chicagoshakes.com
A 500-seat auditorium on Navy Pier makes a fine setting for the works of the Bard. Abridged "Short Shakespeare" and family musicals in summer.
🔲 H8 ✉ 800 E. Grand Avenue ☎ 312/595-5600 🚇 Red Line: Grand 🚌 2, 29, 65, 66, 124

HOUSE OF BLUES
houseofblues.com
Blues and rock from around the world every night. The smaller Back Porch stage has blues nightly and is open at lunch for more of the same. A gospel choir stars at Sunday brunch.
🔲 E9 ✉ 329 N. Dearborn Street ☎ 312/923-2000 🚇 Red Line: Grand 🚌 22, 36

KIBBITZNEST BOOKS, BREWS & BLARNEY
kibbitznest.com
For those ready for a different kind of evening entertainment, head here for beer, wine and board games. Or, grab a book off the book shelves.

A2 · 2212 N. Clybourn Avenue
773/360-7591 · Brown, Purple, Red
Lines: Fullerton · 50, 74

KINGSTON MINES

kingstonmines.com
Regularly voted Chicago's best blues
club, this place has been in business
since 1968. Known for their barbecue,
come here for ribs, Louisiana catfish,
Cajun chicken, jambalaya and other
specialties. Only those in the know
head out here.
C1 · 2548 N. Halsted Street · 773/477-
4646 · Red, Brown Lines: Fullerton · 8,
37, 74

LOGAN SQUARE IMPROV

logansquareimprov.com
Bring your own drinks, $5 and come
early to grab a seat in this intimate,
non-profit storefront theater that offers
improv comedians a stage on which to
ply their craft. Some shows are free to
watch and Wednesdays are open stage
where anyone with or without a group
can perform.
Off map · 2825 W. Diversey Avenue
312/810-7450 · Blue Line: Logan Square
52, 76

LOOKINGGLASS THEATRE

lookingglasstheatre.org
Housed in the Water Tower Pumping
Station, the troupe uses experimental
staging and exciting circus arts.
F7 · 821 N. Michigan Avenue
312/337-0665 · Red Line: Chicago
66, 143, 146, 147, 148, 151

NACIONAL 27

nacional27chicago.com
Guests can dine on modern Latin
cuisine before some tables are removed
to make way for a dance floor. Learn
how to salsa, bachata and tango at the
free Latin dance lessons on Wednesday
nights, from 7.30–8.30pm. DJs and live
bands on weekends.
D7 · 325 W. Huron Street · 312/664-
2727 · Red Line: Chicago · 37

PARK WEST

parkwestchicago.com
The intimate size and strong acoustics
make this the ideal place for music, be
it folk, jazz, rock or something else from
the eclectic program.
D3 · 322 W. Armitage Avenue
773/929-5959 · Brown, Red Lines:
Armitage · 22, 36, 37

ROSA'S LOUNGE

rosaslounge.com
Less touristy than other Chicago blues
clubs, the friendly owners welcome you
to watch intimate shows by talented
blues musicians.
Off map · 3420 W. Armitage Avenue
773/342-0452 · Blue Line: California
73, 82

SPY BAR

spybarchicago.com
Go underground to this clubbing
institution, where the decks have been
spinning since 1995 amid exposed brick
walls and velvet couches. The entrance
is through an alleyway.
E7 · 646 N. Franklin Street · 312/337-
2191 · Brown Line: Chicago · 37

LIQUOR LAWS

Some bars serve liquor until 2am every
night except Saturday, when they may
do so until 3am. Others continue serving
until 4am (5am on Sunday mornings). The
drinking age is 21, and stores may not sell
liquor before noon on Sunday.

NORTH SIDE ENTERTAINMENT AND NIGHTLIFE

STEPPENWOLF THEATRE

steppenwolf.org

Home of the enormously successful Steppenwolf repertory company, founded in 1976, and still a premier venue for the best of Off-Loop theater. The theater has a 900-seat main hall and two smaller spaces for experimental drama. High-profile members include John Malkovich.

🔷 C4 ✉ 1650 N. Halsted Street ☎ 312/335-1650 🚇 Red Line: North/Clybourn 🚌 8, 9, 72

TAO CHICAGO

This complex has gone through so many iterations but today the 1890s sandstone castle-looking building is home to TAO Chicago, a glamorous venue serving high-end Asian cuisine and cocktails, and a posh nightclub.

🔷 E8 ✉ 632 N. Dearborn Street ☎ 224/888-0388 🚇 Red Line: Grand 🚌 22

ZANIES

chicago.zanies.com

A city stalwart, Zanies has been making people laugh for more than 40 years. This intimate comedy club has performances by rising local stars and better-known names.

🔷 E5 ✉ 1548 N. Wells Street ☎ 312/337-4027 🚇 Brown Line: Sedgwick 🚌 9, 72

Where to Eat

PRICES

Prices are approximate, based on a 3-course meal for one person.
$$$$ over $50
$$$ $31–$50
$$ $16–$30
$ up to $15

3 ARTS CLUB CAFÉ ($$$)

restorationhardware.com

This courtyard café is within the chic Restoration Hardware in the Gold Coast.

🔷 E5 ✉ 1300 N. Dearborn Parkway ☎ 312/475-9116 🕒 Daily brunch and dinner 🚇 Red Line: Clark/Division 🚌 22, 36

ALINEA ($$$$)

alinearestaurant.com

Chef Grant Achatz practices a form of modern alchemy at Alinea. This place is for bold and liberal tastes only.

Reservations must be made at least six weeks in advance.

🔷 C4 ✉ 1723 N. Halsted ☎ 312/867-0110 🕒 Daily dinner 🚇 Red Line: North/Clybourn 🚌 8

BRINDILLE ($$$$)

brindille-chicago.com

A French fine-dining restaurant in the River North area. Good wine list.

🔷 E8 ✉ 534 N. Clark Street ☎ 312/595-1616 🕒 Tue–Sat dinner 🚇 Red Line: Grand 🚌 22, 65

EATALY ($–$$$)

eataly.com

Eataly Chicago has restaurants and food counters, two floors of Italian foodstuffs, wine, cheese, breads and a coffee shop.

🔷 F8 ✉ 43 E. Ohio Street ☎ 312/521-8700 🕒 Daily lunch and dinner 🚇 Red Line: Grand 🚌 29, 65

FRONTERA GRILL/ TOPOLOBAMPO ($$$–$$$$)

rickbayless.com/restaurants/frontera-grill

Chef Rick Bayless introduced the nation to regional Mexican food from his Frontera Grill hot spot in River North. Next to it is Topolobampo, its fine-dining counterpart.

🚇 E8 ✉ 445 N. Clark Street ☎ 312/661-1434 🕐 Tue–Fri lunch, Sat brunch and dinner 🚆 Red Line: Grand 🚌 22, 65

GIBSON'S BAR & STEAKHOUSE ($$$$)

gibsonssteakhouse.com

The city's movers and shakers enjoy the steaks and martinis at this classic Chicago steakhouse.

🚇 F6 ✉ 1028 N. Rush Street ☎ 312/266-8999 🕐 Dinner daily 🚆 Red Line: Chicago 🚌 36

GT FISH & OYSTER ($$–$$$)

gtoyster.com

Chef Giuseppe Tentor is a master at this Bib Gourmand-winning seafood restaurant. Expect affordable shared plates and creative cocktails in a hot spot that hasn't lost its fire since it opened in River North.

🚇 E8 ✉ 531 N. Wells Street ☎ 312/929-3501 🕐 Daily dinner 🚆 Brown, Purple Lines: Merchandise Mart 🚌 37, 65, 125

MAGGIANO'S LITTLE ITALY ($$–$$$)

maggianos.com

One of the best and yet best-value Italians in town, which manages to be both smart yet informal, and always busy. Try the baked ziti (a type of pasta) and sausage or lobster ravioli.

🚇 E8 ✉ 516 N. Clark Street ☎ 312/644-7700 🕐 Daily lunch and dinner, Sat–Sun brunch also 🚆 Red Line: Grand 🚌 22, 65

MELI CAFE ($–$$)

melicafe.com

Meli Cafe is a fun and cheery restaurant that serves breakfast dishes, all made using natural, hormone-free and locally grown fresh ingredients, throughout the day.

🚇 E8 ✉ 540 N. Wells Street ☎ 312/527-1850 🕐 Daily breakfast and lunch 🚆 Red Line: Grand 🚌 37, 65, 125

THE PURPLE PIG ($$–$$$)

thepurplepigchicago.com

Chef Jimmy Bannos, Jr. highlights cheese and swine dishes at this Mediterranean restaurant. Located in the heart of the Magnificent Mile, it showcases the flavors of Italy, Greece and Spain.

🚇 F8 ✉ 445 N. Clark Street ☎ 312/464-1744 🕐 Daily lunch and dinner 🚆 Red Line: Grand 🚌 2, 3, 26, 66, 120, 121, 143, 146, 147, 148, 151, 157

RIVA ($$$)

rivanavypier.com

Riva can claim to be Chicago's only waterfront seafood restaurant, with expansive views of the city skyline and Lake Michigan. Though dishes like lobster, king crab, salmon and halibut

---

HOT DOGS

To a Chicagoan, a hot dog is not merely a frank in a bun. The true Chicago hot dog is a Viennese beef sausage smeared with mustard, relish, onions and hot peppers to taste. Brightly lit hot-dog outlets are a feature of the city. Among them are Byron's Hot Dogs:

✉ 1017 W. Irving Park, and other locations ☎ 773/281-7474 🕐 Daily lunch and dinner 🚆 Red line: Sheridan 🚌 80, 151

are popular, Riva also does good steaks in a light and bright smart-casual room.

⊞ H8 ✉ Navy Pier, 700 E. Grand Avenue ☎ 312/644-7482 ⏰ Daily lunch and dinner Ⓖ Red Line: Grand 🚌 2, 29, 65, 66, 124

ROSEBUD ON RUSH ($$$)

rosebudrestaurants.com

With casual dining and a bar downstairs, as well as a restaurant upstairs, Rosebud serves up huge helpings of Italian fare. Menus may include eggplant parmesan or a daily risotto dish, at this and several other city locations.

⊞ F7 ✉ 720 N. Rush Street ☎ 312/266-6444 ⏰ Mon–Fri lunch and dinner, Sat–Sun brunch, lunch and dinner Ⓖ Red Line: Chicago 🚌 66

THE SIGNATURE ROOM AT THE 95TH ($$$$)

signatureroom.com

The Signature Room at the 95th and The Signature Lounge at the 96th are a quintessential Chicago experience. Enjoy fine dining or a cocktail with spectacular skyline views 95 floors above the Magnificent Mile in one of Chicago's architectural gems.

⊞ F7 ✉ 875 N. Michigan Avenue ☎ 312/787-9596 ⏰ Daily lunch and dinner Ⓖ Red Line: Chicago 🚌 125, 143, 146, 147, 148, 151

PIZZA!

Chicago is where the deep-dish pizza was invented, but by who? One contender is Gino's East (locations include ✉ 162 E. Superior Street ☎ 312/266-3337), but Pizzeria Uno (✉ 29 E. Ohio Street ☎ 312/321-1000) also claims to have been first. Stuffed pizzas, with a crust top and bottom, are also a Chicago specialty. For this, try Giordano's (✉ 730 N. Rush Street ☎ 312/951-0747 and other locations).

SPIAGGIA ($$$$)

spiaggiarestaurant.com

Enjoy unforgettable modern Italian dishes at this Michelin-starred fine-dining establishment overlooking Lake Michigan. It is favored by locals and celebrities alike.

⊞ F6 ✉ 980 N. Michigan Avenue ☎ 312/787-9596 ⏰ Daily dinner Ⓖ Red Line: Chicago 🚌 151

STARBUCKS RESERVE ROASTERY ($$)

starbucksreserve.com

The world's largest Starbucks, covering some 43,000sq ft (4,000sq m), offers guests a multisensory experience around coffee. Onsite is a working bakery and rooftop deck, and local mixologists serve specialty cocktails.

⊞ F8 ✉ 646 N. Michigan Avenue ☎ 312/283-7100 ⏰ Mon–Fri 7am–11pm, Sat–Sun 8am–midnight Ⓖ Red Line: Grand 🚌 143, 144, 145, 146, 151

TANTA ($$$)

tantachicago.com

Chef Gastón Acurio produces creative Peruvian dishes served in a beautiful Peru-inspired space. The modern restaurant is also known for its pisco sour cocktail.

⊞ E8 ✉ 118 W. Grand Avenue ☎ 312/222-9700 ⏰ Daily lunch and dinner Ⓖ Red Line: Grand 🚌 156

XOCO ($–$$)

rickbayless.com

This café/restaurant specializes in Mexican churros, caldos, empanadas and tortas. They also make excellent hot chocolate from the cacao bean.

⊞ E8 ✉ 449 N. Clark Street (enter on Illinois Street) ☎ 312/723-2131 ⏰ Tue–Sat breakfast, lunch and dinner Ⓖ Red Line: Grand 🚌 22, 65

South Side

Home to the University of Chicago, the South Side may be the city's most history-rich area but it also looks to the future—it will become the home of former President Barack Obama's presidential library.

Top 25

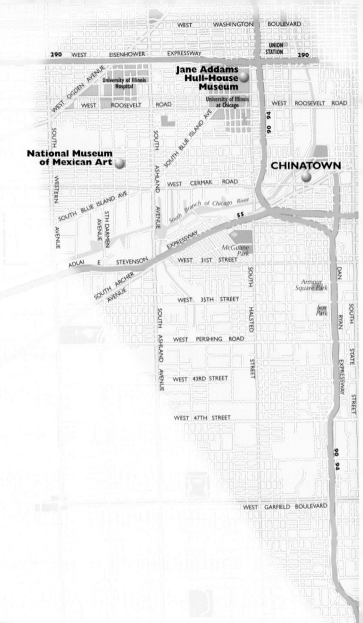

WEST WASHINGTON BOULEVARD

UNION STATION

290 WEST EISENHOWER EXPRESSWAY 290

Jane Addams
Hull-House
Museum

WEST OGDEN AVENUE

University of Illinois
Hospital

WEST ROOSEVELT ROAD

University of Illinois
at Chicago

WEST ROOSEVELT ROAD

94

90

National Museum
of Mexican Art

SOUTH ASHLAND

SOUTH BLUE ISLAND AVE

CHINATOWN

WESTERN AVENUE

SOUTH BLUE ISLAND AVE

5TH DARMEN AVENUE

AVENUE

WEST CERMAK ROAD

South Branch of Chicago River

55

ADLAI E STEVENSON

EXPRESSWAY

McGuane
Park

WEST 31ST STREET

SOUTH ARCHER AVENUE

SOUTH ASHLAND AVENUE

SOUTH

Armour
Square Park

DAN

WEST 35TH STREET

HALSTED

Sox
Park

SOUTH

WEST PERSHING ROAD

STREET

RYAN

STATE STREET

WEST 43RD STREET

EXPRESSWAY

WEST 47TH STREET

90 94

WEST GARFIELD BOULEVARD

0   1 km

0   1 mile

Lake

Michigan

Northerly
Island

Northerly
Island
Park

**Prairie Avenue
District**

55

Burnham
Park

EAST 31ST STREET

EAST 35TH STREET

41

EAST OAKWOOD
BOULEVARD

EAST 47TH STREET

EAST 51ST STREET

EAST HYDE PARK BOULEVARD

Burnham
Park

EAST GARFIELD
BOULEVARD

**DuSable Museum of
African American
History**

**Smart
Museum
of Art**

EAST 55TH
STREET

**Museum
of Science
and Industry**

Washington
Park

**Robie
House**

Oriental
Institute

MIDWAY PLAISANCE

**Biking on
the Chicago
Lakefront**

**University
of Chicago**

EAST 63RD STREET

Jackson
Park

EAST 67TH STREET

Oak Woods
Cemetery

EAST 71ST STREET

SOUTH MICHIGAN AVENUE

SOUTH DR. MARTIN LUTHER KING JR. DRIVE

SOUTH MICHIGAN AVENUE

SOUTH DREXEL BOULEVARD

SOUTH DR. MARTIN LUTHER KING JR. DRIVE

CORNELL DRIVE

SOUTH CORNELL

94

90

Biking on the Chicago Lakefront

TOP
25

Bike riding along the lakefront with the city rising in the background

THE BASICS

chicagoparkdistrict.com/
parks-facilities/lakefront-
trail

➕ See map ▷ 83

✉ Chicago lakefront from
Foster Beach on the north
to 71st Street on the south

♿ Excellent

Bike and Roll Chicago
(bikechicago.com)

✉ Navy Pier, 700 E.
Grand Avenue; Millennium
Park, 239 E. Randolph
Avenue

☎ 312/729-1000

💵 Prices range from
$12.50 per hour or from
$25+ per day, depending
on bike; discounts
available if booking online

HIGHLIGHTS

- 18 miles (29km) of paths
- 25 beaches
- Concession stands in summer
- Views of the skyline
- Bike rentals

Some 18 miles (29km) of paved paths lure walkers, skaters and cyclists to the lakefront, where the South Side offers busy routes and wonderful views.

Bike city Chicago is very bike-friendly, counting over 200 miles (320km) of bike lanes, and closing Lake Shore Drive for one day each summer so that cyclists can enjoy the route exclusively. While the bike lanes on major urban thoroughfares scare the wits out of visitors, the lakefront bike path, free of auto traffic, enchants them. North Side routes are popular and weekend crowds jam the lanes around Oak Street Beach. For a quieter pedal, point your handlebars south and cruise past the Museum Campus or to The 606 (▷ 102), an elevated bike path that winds its way through the Northwestside neighborhoods. On all of these paths, the level terrain is beginner-friendly. Numerous bike sightseeing tours are available, including Bobby's Bike Hike and Bike and Roll Chicago, with two- to three-hour itineraries devoted to the lakefront, neighborhoods or Chicago's signature foods and beers.

Where to find wheels Divvy Bikes, the light-blue rental bikes, can be found all over the city. Rent one for $15 a day, and drop it off at any of their 580 locations. Bike and Roll Chicago also offers several seasonal rental stands in Chicago. The "quadcycle," a four-seater vehicle, only looks fun before you find you are pedaling for the entire family.

Interior of the building (left); African American sculpture exhibit (right)

DuSable Museum of African American History

One of Chicago's unsung museums, this one chronicles aspects of black history, chiefly focusing on African Americans but also encompassing African and Caribbean cultures.

Settlers The museum is named after Chicago's first permanent settler, Jean Baptiste Point du Sable, a Haitian trader born of a French father and African slave mother in whose home the city's first marriage, election and court decision occurred. Further African Americans came in three main waves—during the late 19th century and during the two world wars—settling mostly on Chicago's South Side. Black businesses became established, while the expanding community provided the voter base for the first blacks to enter Chicago politics. Among the settlers were many musicians, and what became Chicago blues was born—an electrified urban form of rural blues fused with elements of jazz. The turbulent 1960s saw growing radicalism among Chicago's African-Americans, and the beginning of the rise to national prominence of South Side politician Jesse Jackson.

Exhibits The first-floor rooms display items from the permanent collection, including the Harold Washington Wing, which chronicles the triumph of Chicago's first black mayor in 1983. There are also meticulously planned temporary exhibitions, while the Arts and Crafts Festival, displaying original works on African-American themes, is held on the second weekend of July.

THE BASICS

dusablemuseum.org
See map ▷ 83
740 E. 56th Place
773/947-0600
Tue–Sat 10–5, Sun 12–5
Red Line: Garfield
59th Street
4, 55
Good
Inexpensive; free on Tue

HIGHLIGHTS

- Slavery exhibit, including shackles
- African functional art, including stools and staffs
- Temporary exhibits devoted to black music, art and history
- Craft fair
- Washington Park setting

Hitting a Blues Club

A performer and the audience at Blue Chicago

HIGHLIGHTS

● Buddy Guy's Legends (▷ 35)
● Blue Chicago (▷ 76)
● Chicago B.L.U.E.S. Bar (▷ 76)
● Kingston Mines (▷ 77)

Southern people moving north in search of jobs in the 1940s amped up the acoustic blues in Chicago, and hearing the music played live is one of the chief attractions of the city.

Blues background Blues music developed among African slaves working southern plantations and descended from "shout outs" of workers in the fields. By the 1920s it developed its signature musical style of repeated three-chord progressions. Vocalists dictate the genre, but performers regularly improvise solos too. Black America's mass exodus from the rural south to the urban north led many musicians to Chicago. The string bands of the Delta region borrowed from jazz groups in the city, amplifying the sound and adding drums, bass, piano and sometimes horns. Innovators Muddy Waters, B.B. King and Buddy Guy established Chicago's electric style, later widely copied by white players like Elvis Presley. The British rock invasion brought the Rolling Stones and Eric Clapton to town to jam with their blues heroes.

A city with the blues Since 1984, on a weekend in early June, marking the opening of summer, the city stages the Chicago Blues Festival, drawing 750,000 listeners to Grant Park. Admission is free and dedicated fest-goers come early with blankets and coolers to stake out a place on the park lawn. The throng can get fairly boozy by evening, but is all-ages-recommended for most of its duration.

Clarke House exterior
(left); main hall in the
Glessner House (right)

Prairie
Avenue District

After the city burned in the Great Fire of 1871, the wealthy and famous moved to the area around Prairie Avenue on the near South Side, where they built elegant mansions, some now open to tours.

From frontier to fancy Hostile American Indians attacked European settlers in this district in what became known as the Fort Dearborn Massacre in 1812. Only after the Great Fire wiped out the city did builders reconsider the site. The who's who of Chicago society built here, including the Fields (of Field Museum fame), the Pullmans (luxury Pullman railroad cars) and the Armours (successful meat-packers). Later generations moved north to the Gold Coast, leaving the Prairie Avenue District to decline. By the mid-20th century many houses were razed, arousing the passions of preservationists who saved most of the 11 remaining Victorian mansions.

Two gems Much of the district provides eye candy for passersby, with the exception of two landmarked buildings open for tours. The oldest, the Greek Revival Clarke House, originally owned by hardware dealer Henry B. Clarke, was actually moved to the area from a location farther south. The more unusual Glessner House is a stand-out in rugged granite with a fortress-like presence on a corner. The interior is considerably warmer, home to Arts and Crafts furnishings, a central courtyard and custom-made art.

THE BASICS

⊞ F14

✉ 1800 and 1900 blocks of S. Prairie Avenue, 1800 block of S. Indiana, and 211–217 E. Cullerton Street

Glessner House Museum

glessnerhouse.org

✉ 1800 S. Prairie Avenue

☎ 312/326-1480

🕐 Tours Wed–Sun at 11.30, 1 and 2.30 (limit 15 people)

🚇 Green Line: Cermack/McCormick then walk

🚌 3, 4

♿ Free on Wed (for Illinois residents only)

Clarke House Museum

✉ 1827 S. Indiana Avenue

🕐 Tours Wed, Fri, Sat at 1 and 2.30 (limit 15 people)

🚇 Green, Orange, Red Lines: Roosevelt

🚌 1, 3, 4

♿ Fair

♿ Free tours on Wed, Fri, Sat at 1 and 2.30

HIGHLIGHTS

● Clarke House
● Glessner House

Museum of Science and Industry

TOP
25

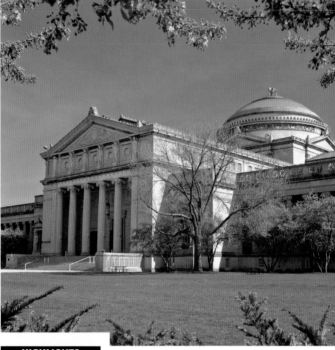

HIGHLIGHTS

- U-505 submarine
- Numbers in Nature: A Mirror Maze
- Genetics and the Baby Chick Hatchery
- Apollo 8 Command Module
- Giant heart
- Giant Dome Theater

TIP

- To avoid lines on the day, order your tickets in advance via the website and have them held at the will-call window.

You can easily spend a day examining the 35,000 artifacts spread across the museum's 14 acres (5.5ha). Hours will pass like minutes as you discover new things about the world—and beyond— at every turn.

Flying high The first eye-catching item is a Boeing 727 attached to an interior balcony. Packed with multimedia exhibits, the plane simulates a flight from San Francisco to Chicago, making full use of flaps, rudders and undercarriage. Reflecting another mode of transportation is the 999 Steam Locomotive, along with other real artifacts including a walk-through 1944 World War II German U-boat and the Apollo 8 spacecraft. The moon-circling Apollo craft forms just a small part of the

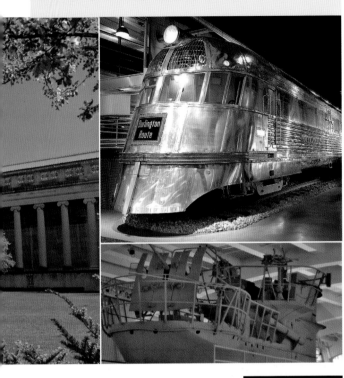

Clockwise from left: Exterior of the Museum of Science and Industry; Pioneer Zephyr; the Conning Tower at the U-505 submarine exhibition

excellent Henry Crown Space Center, housed in an adjoining building.

Medical matters A giant heart that beats to the rhythm of your pulse is among the amazing exhibits detailing the workings of the human body. It's Part of You! The Experience is a multi-faceted exhibit examining the link between the mind, body and spirit. Play Mindball, a relaxation game, and discover how your face will age based on your current habits and your lifestyle.

Industrial issues MSI re-creates a coal mine, complete with a simulated descent to 600ft (180m) in a miners' car. The Farm Tech exhibit allows you to get into a John Deere combine harvester to virtually harvest a cornfield.

THE BASICS

msichicago.org

⊞ See map ▷ 83

✉ 5700 Lake Shore Drive

☎ 773/684-1414

⏰ Daily 9.30–4

🍴 Several cafés

Ⓡ Red and Green Lines: Garfield

🚌 55th, 56th, 57th streets

🚍 6, 15

♿ Excellent

💵 Moderate; see website for free days schedule; separate charge for Giant Dome Theater (▷ 93)

More to See

CHINATOWN

chicagochinatown.org

The ornate Chinatown Gate arching over Cermak at Wentworth marks the heart of Chinatown. Chicago's oldest Chinese district was founded by 19th-century railroad workers. Perhaps the most atmospheric of Chicago's many ethnic enclaves, Chinatown is popular for its many restaurants and streets of stores selling Asian gifts, decorative items, cooking utensils and foods.

🔲 D15 🚇 Red Line: Cermak/Chinatown
🚌 21, 24

JACKSON PARK

In 1893, 27 million people attended the World's Columbian Exposition, in what became Jackson Park, now a fantastic green space with sports courts, a Japanese garden and the Museum of Science and Industry (▷ 88). The park is due to become the home of the Barack Obama Presidential Library and Museum, although there is no set opening date.

🔲 See map ▷ 83 ✉ 6401 S. Stony Island Avenue (between S. Stony Island Avenue and Lake Michigan) 🚇 Red Line: 63rd 🚋 55th, 56th, 57th streets 🚌 6, 15, 28, 63

JANE ADDAMS HULL-HOUSE MUSEUM

hullhousemuseum.org

In the late 19th century, Jane Addams created Hull House, a center in one of the neediest neighborhoods offering English-language and US citizenship courses, child care and other services. The museum is housed in two of the original buildings and features exhibits and various programs throughout the year.

🔲 C11 ✉ 800 S. Halsted Street
☎ 312/413-5353 🕐 Tue–Fri, Sun 9–5
🚇 Blue Line: UIC-Halsted 🚌 8 ♿ Fair
💵 Moderate

NATIONAL MUSEUM OF MEXICAN ART

nationalmuseumofmexicanart.org

Explore Mexican culture through this collection of some 9,000

Japanese Gardens in Jackson Park

seminal pieces by artists of Mexican nationality or descent. Exhibits include prints, photography and paintings as well as sculpture.

⊞ See map ▷ 82 ✉ 1852 W. 19th Street ☎ 312/738-1503 🕐 Tue–Sun 10–5 🚇 Pink Line: 18th Street 🚌 18 ♿ Good 💵 Free

ROBIE HOUSE

flwright.org/visit/robiehouse

A famed example of Frank Lloyd Wright's Prairie School style of architecture, the Frederick C. Robie House was built in 1910. The horizontal emphasis reflects the Midwest's open spaces. Wright designed not only the structure, but all of the interiors and fixtures. Highlights include cantilevered roof eaves and continuous bands of art-glass windows. The museum shop offers a wide variety of items, from pens to furniture.

⊞ See map ▷ 83 ✉ 5757 S. Woodlawn Avenue ☎ 312/994-4000 🕐 Thu–Mon 10–3 🚇 Green Line: Cottage Grove/63rd 🚉 University of Chicago/59th Street 🚌 171, 172, 192 ♿ Few 💵 Moderate

SMART MUSEUM OF ART

smartmuseum.uchicago.edu

Initially run within the University of Chicago's art history department, the Smart Museum of Art features more than 15,000 objects. The collection supports academic and artistic study as well as inspiring new ideas and providing a calm setting for reflection.

⊞ See map ▷ 83 ✉ 5550 S. Greenwood Avenue ☎ 773/702-0200 🕐 Tue–Sun 10–5 (till 8pm Thu) 🚇 Green Line: Garfield 🚌 55, 171, 172 💵 Free

UNIVERSITY OF CHICAGO

uchicago.edu

The oldest buildings on the leafy campus of the University of Chicago are in English Gothic style, but modernists Eero Saarinen and Ludwig Mies van der Rohe added boxier structures in the 1950s and '60s.

⊞ See map ▷ 83 ✉ Campus is largely bounded by Blackstone Avenue, Cottage Grove, 55th Street and 59th Street 🚇 Green Line: Garfield 🚌 55, 171, 172

Robie House

South Side Shuffle

The best place for a walk on the South Side is between Lake Michigan and the University of Chicago.

DISTANCE: Approximately 2.5 miles (4km) **ALLOW:** 2 hours

START

MSI (▷ 88) 🚇 Red, Green Lines: Garfield 🚌 6, 15

END

WOODLAWN TAP (▷ 93) 🚇 Red, Green Lines: Garfield 🚌 55, 171, 172

1 Begin with a look at the Museum of Science and Industry. The place is so vast it could easily take your whole day.

2 Exit the museum on the south side facing the Jackson Park Lagoon, created by New York's famed Central Park designer Frederick Law Olmsted for the world's fair.

3 Loop the shore on the east side of the Lagoon until you are opposite the museum, where North Bridge leads to Wooded Island and the lovely restored Osaka Japanese Garden.

4 Leave Jackson Park heading west along Midway Plaisance, and continue for several blocks to Woodlawn.

8 Walk north on Ellis Avenue three blocks until you reach 55th Street. Take a right and continue to the Woodlawn Tap for refreshments.

7 Walk one block west on 58th Street, passing the Oriental Institute, to reach the main quadrangle of the University of Chicago campus (▷ 91). Admire Cobb Hall and Bond Chapel.

6 Continue north on Woodlawn one block to admire the Robie House (▷ 91), designed by Frank Lloyd Wright and open for tours.

5 At Woodlawn and 59th Street just opposite the Midway, pop into the Rockefeller Memorial Chapel.

SOUTH SIDE WALK

Entertainment and Nightlife

COURT THEATRE

courttheatre.org

The University of Chicago's theater has been staging high-quality dramas and musicals for more than 50 years and is highly regarded for its fine acting and innovative stagings.

➕ Off map ✉ 5535 W. Ellis Avenue ☎ 773/753-4472 🚇 Green Line: Garfield 🚌 55, 171, 172

GIANT DOME THEATER

msichicago.org

One of only two in the world, the Giant Dome Theater is MSI's state-of-the-art laser projection screen that helps bring scientific adventures to life. Timed entry fee payable for movies.

➕ Off map ✉ 5700 S. Street and Lake Shore Drive ☎ 773/684-1414 🚇 Red and Green Lines: Garfield 🚌 6, 15 💲 Expensive

THE PROMONTORY

promontorychicago.com

Dance or just sit and listen to the live soul, jazz, afro fusion, hip-hop and other black-rooted music in this popular full-service bar. Tickets are needed for some shows. Check out the wall of vinyl albums in the entrance, signed by the artists who have performed there.

➕ Off map ✉ 5311 S. Lake Park Avenue West ☎ 312/801-2100 🚇 51st/53rd Hyde Park 🚌 15, 28

REGGIE'S CHICAGO

reggieslive.com

Reggie's Music Joint is a bar and grill that also puts on a full range of live music, from punk and indie to homegrown Chicago jazz and blues. There's also a menu of salads, sandwiches, burgers and TV dinners—served on silver foil trays. There are 25 draft beers too, even more by the bottle. In good weather, spacious Reggie's Trainwreck Rooftop Deck has a bar, 8 flat screens, a free pool table and more.

➕ F15 ✉ 2105 S. State Street ☎ 312/949-0120 🚇 Red and Green Lines: Cermack 🚌 21, 29

SOUTH CHICAGO DANCE THEATRE

southchicagodancetheatre.com

South Chicago Dance Theatre might have launched in 2017 but many of the company's collaborators have been part of the South Side's arts community since the 1960s. Performances include classical and contemporary dance styles.

➕ Off map ✉ 5540 S. Hyde Park Boulevard ☎ 708/906-7237 🚇 Green Line: Cottage Grove/63rd Street 🚌 6, 28, 55

WOODLAWN TAP

Chicago is famed for its neighborhood taverns, corner taps that serve as places where communities gather and bind. Hyde Park lacks the saloons of other neighborhoods, but the Woodlawn Tap, also known as "Jimmy's," goes a long way to fill in, with three dimly lit rooms filled with punters deep in conversation.

➕ Off map ✉ 1172 E. 55th Street ☎ 773/643-5516 🚇 Red, Green Lines: Garfield 🚌 55, 171, 172

CHINESE NEW YEAR

In January or early February, thousands of visitors flock to Chinatown to celebrate Chinese New Year. The parade features dragon dancers, martial artists and Chinese dancers as well as the incongruous bagpipe marching band and assorted politicians. The route runs through the heart of the neighborhood on Wentworth from Cermak to 24th Street. Afterward, parade-goers jam the area's many restaurants for dim sum.

Where to Eat

5 RABANITOS RESTAURANTE & TAQUERIA ($$)

5rabanitosdotcom.wordpress.com

Enjoy tacos, guacamole and some of the most flavorful Mexican dishes at this colorful restaurant in the heart of Pilsen. Also includes plenty of vegetarian options. It's a BYO place—bring your own alcohol.

Off map ⊠ 1758 W. 18th Street ☎ 312/285-2710 ⏰ Tue–Sun lunch and dinner, Sat–Sun brunch 🚇 Pink Line: 18th 🚌 18

CHICAGO'S HOME OF CHICKEN AND WAFFLES ($)

chicagoschickenandwaffles.com

Whether it's a late-night feast or an after-church breakfast, people crave the soul food at this Bronzeville spot. While they're best known for their fried chicken and waffles, fans also rave about the catfish dishes.

Off map ⊠ 3947 S. King Drive ☎ 773/536-3300 ⏰ Daily breakfast, lunch and dinner 🚇 Green Line: Indiana 🚌 3

FLO & SANTOS ($–$$)

floandsantos.com

The menu at this informal restaurant mixes Italian and Polish favorites, sometimes in the same dish. The specialty pizzas are excellent too.

F13 ⊠ 1310 S. Wabash Avenue ☎ 312/566-9817 ⏰ Daily lunch and dinner; from 9am on Chicago Bear game days 🚇 Red, Orange, Green Lines: Roosevelt 🚌 3, 4, 146

MANNY'S DELI & CAFETERIA ($)

mannysdeli.com

Corned beef and pastrami sandwiches are piled high, with a potato pancake and pickle on the side, at this landmark Jewish deli. Grab a tray and move down the cafeteria line.

D12 ⊠ 1141 S. Jefferson Street ☎ 312/939-2855 ⏰ Tue–Sat 7am–8pm, Mon 7–3, Sun 8–3 🚇 Blue Line: Clinton 🚌 12, 18

LA PETITE FOLIE ($$$)

lapetitefolie.com

A rare, fine-dining outpost in Hyde Park, La Petite Folie serves unfussy French food. It's a popular precurtain spot for Court Theatre patrons.

Off map ⊠ 1504 E. 55th Street ☎ 773/493-1394 ⏰ No lunch Sat–Sun; closed Mon 🚇 Green Line: Garfield 🚌 55

PHOENIX ($$)

chinatownphoenix.com

Enjoy panoramic views of the Chicago skyline here at Phoenix, along with delicious dim sum. Many of the waiters do not speak English; good humor and the pointing method of ordering prevail. Due to its popularity, long waits are common on weekends.

D15 ⊠ 2131 S. Archer Avenue ☎ 312/328-0848 ⏰ Daily breakfast, lunch and dinner 🚇 Red Line: Cermak/Chinatown 🚌 21, 24

SWEET MAPLE CAFE ($$)

sweetmaplecafe.com

Sweet Maple Cafe, a place dripping with Southern country charm, is the spot for breakfast or brunch if you love dishes like biscuits made from scratch and cinnamon roll pancakes.

A12 ⊠ 1339 W. Taylor Street ☎ 312/243-8908 ⏰ Mon–Fri breakfast and lunch, Sat–Sun breakfast only 🚇 Bue Line: Racine 🚌 157

Farther Afield

Ironically one of Chicago's top tourist sights isn't even in the city. Frank Lloyd Wright's home and original office is in Oak Park. Venture off the beaten path and into the neighborhoods to get a feel for life outside the city limits.

Top 25

NILES

GROVE

SKOKIE

Olympia
Park

Caldwell
Woods

Chicago River North Branch

NORTH

NORTHWEST

HIGHWAY

Indian Road
Woods

EDENS

WEST

EXPRESSWAY

94

WEST

41

NORTH

LINCOLN

TOUHY

DEVON

AVENUE

North Shore Channel

21

← Chicago O'Hare
International
Airport

171

90

WEST

PETERSON

AVENUE

LaBagh Woods

WEST

FOSTER

AVENUE

Ronan
Park

JOHN

F

KENNEDY

Horner
Park

19

WEST

IRVING

PARK

ROAD

19

California
Park

NORRIDGE

Hiawatha
Park

WEST

NORTH

BELMONT

AVENUE

NORTH

MILWAUKEE

NORTH

EXPRESSWAY

AVENUE

ELMWOOD
PARK

Riis
Park

CENTRAL

50

Des Plaines River

WEST

GRAND

AVENUE

Hanson
Park

43

64

WEST

NORTH

AVENUE

PULASKI

The 606

Humboldt
Park

Frank Lloyd Wright
Home and Studio,
Frank Lloyd Wright Tour

Thatcher
Woods

FIRST

Ernest
Hemingway
Museum

OAK
PARK

WEST

CHICAGO

AVENUE

ROAD

AVENUE

Garfield Park
Conservatory

Maywood
Park

WEST

SOUTH

MADISON

STREET

Garfield
Park

MAYWOOD

290

WEST

EISENHOWER

EXPRESSWAY

BROADVIEW

Miller
Meadow

WEST

ROOSEVELT

ROAD

RIDGELAND

SOUTH

Douglas
Park

HARLEM

BERWYN

WEST

CERMAK

ROAD

Cook County
Forest Preserve

AVENUE

AVENUE

CICERO

CICERO

SOUTH

Brookfield
Zoo

NORTH
RIVERSIDE

WEST

OGDEN

AVENUE

AVENUE

34

43

BROOKFIELD

Chicago Sanitary and Ship Canal

ADLAI

STEVENSON

EXPRESSWAY

55

SOUTH

PULASKI

SOUTH

KEDZIE

55

WEST

47TH

STREET

ROAD

171

SOUTH

ARCHER

AVENUE

ROAD

WEST

ARCHER

AVENUE

Chicago Midway
International
Airport

63RD

STREET

50

WEST

Balzekas
Museum of
Lithuanian
Culture

Marquette
Park

0   1 km
0   1 mile

Interior of Stitch (opposite); shoppers delight in the variety of stores here

Boutique Browsing in Wicker Park/Bucktown

West of the Gold Coast, following North Avenue, a progressive, urban neighborhood emerges. This gentrifying area is a hub for artists and musicians, and contains many new restaurants and a growing range of shops. Festivals and a farmers' market bring in crowds from spring through fall.

History In the mid-1850s Irish immigrants settled around the Rolling Mill Steel Works. Businesses lined the commercial avenues and homes were tucked in streets behind them. After the Great Fire of 1871 the area boomed as the well-heeled built spacious Victorian mansions. Waves of immigration followed, running along Milwaukee Avenue. From the 1930s to the 1970s the area declined, but in the 1980s Wicker Park and Bucktown took off as shops, clubs and restaurants all moved in.

Where to shop Both vintage and on-trend fashions are on show at the boutique Una Mae's (1528 N. Milwaukee Avenue). P.45 (1643 N. Damen Avenue) and Moon Voyage (2010 W. Pierce Avenue) showcase women's clothing, accessories and jewelry. Matty & Lou (1730 W. Division Street) stocks high-end looks at affordable prices. For gifts, Paperish Mess (1945 W. Chicago Avenue) features jewelry, stationery, art prints and more from hundreds of makers and designers, while Neighborly (1909 W. Division Street) offers home goods including pieces by Midwestern designers.

THE BASICS

wickerparkbucktown.com

⊞ See map ▷ 97

✉ The center of the neighborhood is at the three-way intersection of Milwaukee, Damen and North avenues

🕐 Most shops Mon–Sat 11–7, Sun 12–5

Ⓑ Blue Line: Damen

🚍 50, 56, 72

HIGHLIGHTS

● Matty & Lou
● Moon Voyage
● Neighborly
● Paperish Mess
● P.45

FARTHER AFIELD TOP 25

Frank Lloyd Wright Home and Studio

The Children's Playroom (left); the exterior of Frank Lloyd Wright's Studio (right)

THE BASICS

flwright.org

⊞ See map ▷ 96

✉ 951 Chicago Avenue, Oak Park

☎ 312/994-4000

🕓 Guided tours only:
Mar–Dec daily 10–4;
Jan–Feb 10–3

🚇 Green Line: Oak Park Avenue

🚉 Oak Park

🚌 309, 313

♿ Few

💵 Moderate

HIGHLIGHTS

● Barrel-vaulted playroom
● Drafting Room with chain harness system to support the roof
● Stained-glass leaded windows
● Skylights
● Wright-designed furniture

TIP

● Advanced tickets are highly recommended. Get them up to midnight the night before the tour from the website.

The Frank Lloyd Wright Home and Studio provides an insight into the early ideas of one of the greatest and most influential architects of the 20th century.

Organic ideas Working for the Chicago-based architect Louis Sullivan, the 22-year-old Frank Lloyd Wright designed this home in 1889 for himself, his first wife and their children, and furnished it with pieces he designed. The shingled exterior is not typical of Wright, but the bold geometric shape stands out among the neighboring Queen Anne-style houses. Inside, the open-plan, central fireplaces and low ceilings are the earliest examples of the elements that became fundamental in Wright's so-called Prairie School of Architecture. Notable are the children's playroom, the high-backed chairs in the dining room and the willow tree that grows through the walls in keeping with Wright's theory of organic architecture—architecture in harmony with its surroundings.

Prairie views In 1893, Wright opened his own practice in an annex to the house: A concealed entrance leads into an office showcasing many of Wright's ideas, such as suspended lamps and an open-plan work space. The draftsmen once employed here on seminal Prairie School buildings worked in a stunningly designed room in sight of what was then prairie. Wright's disciples designed 125 buildings here, including the nearby Unity Temple and the Robie House (▷ 91) in Hyde Park on Chicago's South Side.

Aerial view of Wrigley Field (left); welcoming fans to the ballpark (right)

Wrigley Field

Wrigley Field is home to the Chicago Cubs, an integral part of the team's identity, and a beloved city landmark. Loyal Cubs fans were finally rewarded with a World Series Championship in 2016—their first in 108 years.

Landmark With its ivy-covered brick outfield wall, Wrigley Field provides the perfect setting for America's traditional pastime. Built in 1914, the ballpark has resisted artificial turf, and the game takes place on grass within an otherwise ordinary city neighborhood, affectionately known as Wrigleyville. With limited car-parking in the area, most fans have to use public transportation to reach the ballpark. General admission bleacher seating overlooking the outfield is popular at Wrigley Field. Dedicated Cubs fans withstand the vagaries of Chicago weather, which during the March to September season can encompass anything from snow to sunshine and 100°F (38°C) temperatures.

Tradition Above the seats is the much-loved 1937 scoreboard on which the numbers are moved not by computer but by human hands. Fans stand in the middle of the seventh inning and sing "Take Me Out to the Ballgame," often led by a visiting celebrity and accompanied by a live organist. Today, the baseball field includes two huge video boards which show replays, statistics and team history. Rooftops across the street from the ballpark have been converted to allow fans to watch the game.

THE BASICS

cubs.com
✚ See map ▷ 97
✉ 1060 W. Addison Street
☎ 773/404-2827
🕐 Games: Mar–Sep
🍴 Fast-food stands
🚇 Red Line: Addison
🚌 22, 151
♿ Good
🎟 Tickets moderate to expensive

HIGHLIGHTS

● Outfield wall covered in ivy
● Bleacher seats
● Hand-operated scoreboard
● Seventh-inning stretch

More to See

THE 606
the606.org
The 606 is an exciting 2.7-mile (4.3km) elevated bike path that takes you over streets, past houses and parks and through the Northwestside neighborhoods. With lots of on/off ramps, it's easy to stop and sample the area's shops and cafés. Bike rentals are at each end of the path.
🞤 See map ▷ 96–97 ✉ Bloomingdale Road, between Ashland and Ridgeway ⏰ Daily 6am–11pm 🚇 Blue Line: Western, Damen 🚌 X49, 72, 73

BOYSTOWN
northalsted.com
The pocket of Lakeview around North Halsted Street from Belmont north to Addison is the focus of the LGBTQ+ community in Chicago, and has a collection of bars and some good restaurants.
🞤 See map ▷ 97 ✉ Halsted Street from Belmont north to Addison 🚇 Red Line: Belmont Addison; Brown Line: Belmont 🚌 8, 77 ♿ Good

ERNEST HEMINGWAY MUSEUM
ehfop.org
This museum features collections remembering the Nobel Prize-winning writer who spent his first 18 years in Oak Park. Hemingway's birthplace, a Queen Anne home that was built in 1890 and the first home in Oak Park to have electricity, is open the same hours as the museum.
🞤 See map ▷ 96 ✉ 339 N. Oak Park Avenue ☎ 708/445-3071 ⏰ Sat 10–5, Wed–Fri, Sun 1–5 🚇 Green Line: Oak Park 🚂 Oak Park 🚌 90, 309, 313 ♿ Few 💵 Inexpensive

FRANK LLOYD WRIGHT TOUR
flwright.org
The Oak Park neighborhood around Wright's former home and studio hosts 26 Wright-designed homes—the largest concentration of the architect's buildings in the world. Take the tour after visiting the Frank Lloyd Wright Home and Studio (▷ 100), which will show you the Prairie School style.
🞤 See map ▷ 96 ✉ 951 Chicago Avenue ☎ 708/848-1976 🚇 Green Line: Oak Park Avenue 🚌 90, 309, 313 ♿ Few 💵 Moderate

GARFIELD PARK CONSERVATORY
garfieldconservatory.org
The conservatory has 5 acres (2ha) of tropical and subtropical plants. Highlights include collections of palms, ferns and cacti. Chicagoans come here for gardening tips and to remind them that winter does end.
🞤 See map ▷ 96 ✉ 300 N. Central Park Avenue ☎ 773/638-1766 ⏰ Daily 9–5, (Wed till 8pm). Extended hours for shows 🚇 Green Line: Conservatory/Central Park 🚌 66, 82 ♿ Few 💵 Free

GRACELAND CEMETERY AND ARBORETUM
gracelandcemetery.org
Covering some 120 acres (50ha), Graceland is the resting place of famous and infamous Chicagoans. Louis Sullivan is here, as are other Chicago architects. The free map from the office is essential.
🞤 See map ▷ 97 ✉ 4001 N. Clark Street ☎ 773/525-1105 ⏰ Mon–Fri 8–4, Sat–Sun 9–4 (until 6 daily in summer) 🚇 Brown Line: Irving Park; Red Line: Sheridan 🚌 80 ♿ Good 💵 Free

Shopping

THE ALLEY

thealleychicago.com

If your idea of an accessory is a classic Zippo lighter or a Che Guevara belt buckle, the Alley store, alternative clothing stockist, is the place to find it, plus leather jackets and motorcycle boots.

✉ 843 W. Belmont Avenue ☎ 773/883-1800 🚇 Brown, Red Lines: Belmont 🚌 77

BARI ZAKI STUDIO

barizaki.com

A darling boutique dedicated to the art of bookbinding, handmade papers and drawing instruments.

✉ 3858 N. Lincoln Avenue ☎ 773/294-7766 🚇 Brown Line: Irving Park 🚌 80

BROADWAY ANTIQUES MARKET

bamchicago.com

The 75-plus antique dealers at this two-floor antiques haven sell everything from art deco to mid-20th-century modern pieces.

✉ 6130 N. Broadway Avenue ☎ 773/743-5444 🚇 Red Line: Granville 🚌 36

ENJOY LINCOLN SQUARE

enjoylincolnsquare.com

This is a trendy shop within the very walkable Lincoln Square neighborhood that sells unique gifts, toys, books and greeting cards as well as items for the home and office.

✉ 4723 N. Lincoln Avenue ☎ 773/334-8626 🚇 Brown Line: Western 🚌 49, 81

HAZEL APPAREL AND GIFTS

hazelchicago.com

This Ravenswood neighborhood boutique has become a local favorite for contemporary women and men's clothing, jewelry and gifts.

✉ 1926 W. Montrose Avenue ☎ 773/904-7779 🚇 Brown Line: Montrose 🚌 78

SAINT ALFRED

stalfred.com

A small store, Saint Alfred features men's and women's footwear and sneakers (tennies) from many different brands, as well as streetwear.

✉ 1531 N. Milwaukee Avenue ☎ 773/486-7159 🚇 Blue Line: Damen 🚌 56

UNABRIDGED BOOKSTORE

unabridgedbookstore.com

Chicago's leading LGBTQ+ bookstore and a rare independent bookseller offers publications on a wide array of topics. Well-read and knowledgable employees offer their personal touts for books they like, so look out for their notes attached to the racks.

✉ 3251 N. Broadway ☎ 773/883-9119 🚇 Brown, Red, Purple Lines: Belmont 🚌 36, 77, 151, 156

WOLFBAIT & B-GIRLS

wolfbaitchicago.com

Affordable clothing, gifts, stationery, personal care items and jewelry, all handmade by Chicago designers, can be found in this cozy boutique across from Logan Square Park.

✉ 3131 W. Logan Boulevard ☎ 312/698-8685 🚇 Blue Line: Logan Square 🚌 56

WOMEN & CHILDREN FIRST BOOKSTORE

womenandchildrenfirst.com

Since 1979, this indie bookshop has aimed to celebrate and amplify under-represented voices. It's become one of the largest feminist bookstores in the country, stocking more than 30,000 books by and about women, children's books, as well as LGBTQ+ fiction and non-fiction.

✉ 5233 N. Clark Street ☎ 773/769-9299 🚇 Red Line: Berwyn 🚌 22, 92

Entertainment and Nightlife

BEAT KITCHEN

beatkitchen.com

A smallish but popular venue, the Beat Kitchen makes a good setting for folk and rock acts, predominantly from around Chicago.

✉ 2100 W. Belmont Avenue ☎ 773/281-4444 🚇 Brown, Red Lines: Belmont 🚌 77

CUBBY BEAR

cubbybear.com

Its location opposite Wrigley Field makes this sports bar a favorite spot for post-Cubs games. The live music spans rock, country, reggae and blues, plus dancing and beer.

✉ 1059 W. Addison Street ☎ 773/327-1662 🚇 Red Line: Addison 🚌 22, 152

GREEN MILL COCKTAIL LOUNGE

greenmilljazz.com

This classic Uptown jazz club dates back to Chicago's Prohibition days when it was known as a speakeasy. It is home to the Sunday-night Uptown Poetry Slam, an open-mic night for performance poets, and has spawned imitators the world over.

✉ 4802 N. Broadway Avenue ☎ 773/878-5552 🚇 Red Line: Lawrence 🚌 36, 81

MARTYRS

martyrslive.com

A showcase place for up-and-coming musicians and comedians, there's always a fun live show going on at this bar, a favorite among locals.

✉ 3855 N. Lincoln Avenue ☎ 773/404-9494 🚇 Brown Line: Irving Park 🚌 50

METRO

metrochicago.com

Major mid-size venue for live rock, with ample space for dancing and plentiful seating with good views.

RAVINIA FESTIVAL

From mid-June to Labor Day, the northern suburb of Highland Park plays host to the Ravinia Festival. The summer home of the Chicago Symphony Orchestra, Ravinia also stages rock and jazz concerts, dance events and other cultural activities. Festival goers drive the 25 miles (40km) from central Chicago; you can also get there by commuter train. Details ☎ 847/433–8819; ravinia.org.

✉ 3730 N. Clark Street ☎ 773/549-4140 🚇 Red Line: Addison 🚌 22, 152

MUSIC BOX THEATRE

musicboxtheatre.com

Independent, classic and foreign films fill the slate at this 1929 Lakeview movie palace with twinkling stars in the ceiling and an organist employed to play during holiday sing-alongs.

✉ 3733 N. Southport Avenue ☎ 773/871-6604 🚇 Brown Line: Southport 🚌 9, 152

OLD TOWN SCHOOL OF FOLK MUSIC

oldtownschool.org

Set in "restaurant row" of the Lincoln Square neighborhood, this folk and world music venue hosts concerts in an intimate setting. The school also offers music lessons with instruments ranging from the ukelele to Qi Gong (chi kung).

✉ 4544 N. Lincoln Avenue ☎ 773/728-6000 🚇 Brown Line: Western 🚌 11, 49

THE WILD HARE

wildharemusic.com

Top-notch live reggae and other Caribbean and African sounds in the heart of Wrigleyville.

✉ 2610 N. Halsted Street ☎ 773/770-3511 🚇 Brown, Purple, Red Lines: Fullerton 🚌 8

Where to Eat

ARUN'S ($$$$)

arunsthai.com

Superb Thai fare, with subtle spicing reflecting the exceptional talent in the kitchen. Tasting menus only.

✉ 4156 N. Kedzie Avenue ☎ 773/539-1909 🕐 Dinner only; closed Mon 🚇 Brown Line: Kedzie 🚌 78, 80

GALIT ($$–$$$)

galitrestaurant.com

Located in the heart of Lincoln Park, Galit brings a chef-driven Middle Eastern menu to those who love sharing flavorful dishes and enjoying creative cocktails in a trendy setting.

✉ 2429 N. Lincoln Avenue ☎ 773/360-8755 🕐 Tue–Sun dinner 🚇 Brown, Purple and Red Lines: Fullerton 🚌 8, 37, 74

GIRL & THE GOAT ($$$)

girlandthegoat.com

Executive Chef Stephanie Izard, a Bravo's Top Chef winner, serves everything from the wildly popular sautéed green beans to goat empanadas at her West Loop restaurant.

✉ 809 W. Randolph Street ☎ 312/492-6262 🕐 Daily dinner 🚇 Green and Pink Lines: Morgan 🚌 8

NOON-O-KABAB ($$)

noonokabab.com

Feast on the large, budget-friendly portions of fresh, authentic Persian food at this homey restaurant, in one of Chicago's Middle Eastern neighborhoods. Specialties include their seasonal kebabs, warm pita bread, char-boiled vegetables and dill rice.

✉ 4701 N. Kedzie Avenue ☎ 773/279-8899 🕐 Daily lunch and dinner 🚇 Brown Line: Kedzie 🚌 81, 93

SMOQUE BBQ ($–$$)

smoquebbq.com

Follow your nose and you'll smell the sweet scent of BBQ before passing the doors of this popular BBQ outpost. It is known for its slinging ribs, brisket and pulled pork.

✉ 3800 N. Pulaski Road ☎ 773/545-7427 🕐 Tue–Sun lunch and dinner 🚇 Blue Line: Irving Park 🚌 53

TANGO SUR ($$–$$$)

tangosurgrill.com

Expect a wait, which is worth it, at this candlelit Argentinian steakhouse in Lakeview. Perfect for a romantic evening or out with friends. The restaurant is BYOB, but you can enjoy a cocktail or pick up a bottle of something to drink at Bodego Sur next door.

✉ 3763 N. Southport Avenue ☎ 773/477-5466 🕐 Dinner daily; lunch Sun 🚇 Brown Line: Southport 🚌 9, 80

INDIA IN CHICAGO

Chicago's Indian community thrives along Devon Avenue on the far North Side of the city. Bollywood video stores and sari shops occasionally intersperse the long string of restaurants that line either side of the street west of Western Avenue. Top choices include Tiffin (✉ 2536 W. Devon Avenue ☎ 773/338-2143) and Hema's Kitchen (✉ 2439 W. Devon Avenue ☎ 773/338-1627). Many places feature a bargain-price buffet for the midday meal.

Chicago's hotels are largely clustered downtown within walking distance of shopping, restaurants, nightlife and museums. Lodgings near to O'Hare Airport cater primarily to business travelers.

Introduction

Chicago's hotels concentrate in the tourist regions downtown, but within that region, where you stay depends very much on what you aim to do.

An Experience
If it's shopping you seek, look for something on the near North Side or along the Magnificent Mile. Loop district hotels plant you closest to many top cultural attractions, including the Art Institute of Chicago and Randolph Street theaters. River North hotels provide great access to restaurants and nightlife. To experience life as a Chicago resident you might try something in close proximity to Wrigley Field or the Lincoln Park Zoo.

For Your Own Budget
Most of the city's luxury and boutique hotels tend to be located on or near the Magnificent Mile, offering easy access to high-end shops. Mid-range hotels are scattered throughout the Loop, River North and near North Side regions. Budget hotels tend to be near the margins of downtown or in North Side neighborhoods such as Lakeview.

Best Times to Visit
Because business travel is so vital to hoteliers, many of them drop their rates to lure in weekend guests. You probably won't find such bargains in the height of summer, but during the off-season the sales can be dramatic.

DATES TO AVOID

Chicago has the biggest convention center in the country, McCormick Place. Some conventions swell to take every hotel room in the region. Others, such as the National Restaurant Show each May, make getting a restaurant reservation difficult. Business travelers account for 55 percent of hotel business downtown. September, October, November and May are big convention months. If crowds concern you, phone ahead when booking your hotel and ask about group business during your stay.

Budget Hotels

PRICES

Expect to pay between $75 and $150 for a budget hotel.

BEST WESTERN HAWTHORNE TERRACE

hawthorneterrace.com

Wrigley Field is a short walk from this 59-room neighborhood inn with nice-for-the-price amenities including WiFi and a fitness center. The hotel is also close to Wrigleyville and North Halsted restaurant scene, as well as the Lincoln Park lakefront.

➕ Off map at C1 ✉ 3434 N. Broadway ☎ 773/244-3434 🚇 Red Line: Addison 🚌 36

HOTEL VERSEY

hotelversey.com

Each of the rooms in this hotel near the lakefront, and 3 miles (5km) north of the Loop, features bold designs and local art. The hotel is on a busy street intersection and is surrounded by restaurants and shopping. There are train and bus stops close by.

➕ C1 ✉ 644 W. Diversey ☎ 773/525-7010 🚇 Brown, Purple Lines: Diversey 🚌 22, 36, 76

MOXY

marriott.com/hotels/travel/chiox-moxy-chicago-downtown

A contemporary hotel located in the heart of River North and near the Magnificent Mile. The hotel has a 24/7 taco window, free WiFi and 49" smart TVs. There is a bar serving custom cocktails and a 24-hour gym as well as a convenience store.

➕ E8 ✉ 530 N. LaSalle Drive ☎ 312/527-7200 🚇 Red Line: Grand; Brown, Purple Lines: Merchandise Mart 🚌 65, 156

OHIO HOUSE

ohiohousemotel.com

This dependable, simple motel has 50 rooms and offers exceptionally good rates in a River North location. Free parking and WiFi.

➕ E8 ✉ 600 N. LaSalle Street ☎ 312/943-6000 🚇 Red Line: Grand 🚌 156

THE RIVER HOTEL

chicagoriverhotel.com

Located across the Chicago River, this contemporary hotel is a short walk from Millennium Park and the Magnificent Mile. Some rooms have microwaves and minifridges, and there is an on-site fitness room and business center.

➕ F9 ✉ 75 E. Wacker Drive ☎ 312/777-0990 🚇 Brown, Orange, Purple, Pink and Green Lines: State/Lake 🚌 2, 6, 134, 135, 136, 146, 148

THE ST. CLAIR HOTEL— MAGNIFICENT MILE

thestclairmagnificentmile.com

In a red-brick building, the St. Clair Hotel is just minutes away from the Museum of Contemporary Art and two blocks from the Magnificent Mile. It's also pet-friendly.

➕ F8 ✉ 162 E. Ontario Street ☎ 312/787-3580 🚇 Red Line: Grand 🚌 2, 3, 26, 125, 143, 146, 147, 148, 151, 157

B&BS

Bed-and-breakfasts are typically Victorian homes fitted out in sumptuous style and filled with antiques. They span all price categories and there is a particularly strong concentration in Oak Park. Chicago Bed and Breakfast Association (Chicago-bed-breakfast.com) operates a reservation system; it handles properties that are usually centrally located.

Mid-Range Hotels

ACME HOTEL
acmehotelcompany.com
Filled with modern pop art, this boutique hotel seems more expensive than it is, especially for a downtown hotel. Hi-tech amenities and check-ins appeal to young travelers, and so does their new ski lodge-like bar with a hot tub.
➕ F8 ✉ 15 E. Ohio Street ☎ 312/894-0800 🚇 Red Line: Grand 🚌 36, 65

COURTYARD BY MARRIOTT
marriott.com
The Loop is adjacent to this Marriott hotel so, unsurprisingly, the 337 comfortable, large rooms here are very popular with business travelers.
➕ F8 ✉ 30 E. Hubbard Street ☎ 312/329-2500 🚇 Red Line: Grand 🚌 36

EMBASSY SUITES
embassysuiteschicago.com
The 367 suites are in a good location for Michigan Avenue shopping and River North nightlife. Substantial buffet breakfast and a free evening cocktail party included.
➕ E8 ✉ 600 N. State Street ☎ 312/943-3800 🚇 Red Line: Grand 🚌 36, 125

THE GODFREY HOTEL
godfreyhotelchicago.com
This contemporary yet comfortable hotel, in a quiet area north of down-town, has a modern vibe, free WiFi and a killer view from its stylish rooftop bar.
➕ D7 ✉ 127 W. Huron Street ☎ 312/649-2000 🚇 Red, Brown and Purple Lines: Chicago 🚌 22, 156

HAMPTON INN CHICAGO DOWNTOWN/MAGNIFICENT MILE
hamptoninn3.hilton.com
This Hampton Inn is good value, since it includes free WiFi and a complimentary breakfast. The downtown/Magnificent Mile location has a seasonal rooftop pool plus business and fitness centers.
➕ F7 ✉ 160 E. Huron Street ☎ 312/706-0888 🚇 Red Line: Chicago 🚌 3, 26, 125, 143, 146, 147, 148, 151

HOMEWOOD SUITES BY HILTON
homewoodsuiteschicago.com
These comfortable apartment rooms are some of the best value in town; break-fast included, free WiFi, business center access, a pool and fitness center, and complimentary snacks and drinks four nights a week.
➕ F7 ✉ 40 East Grand Avenue ☎ 312/644-2222 🚇 Red Line: Grand 🚌 29, 65

HOTEL ALLEGRO
allegrochicago.com
This well-established Loop hotel, known for its whimsical yet luxurious decor, welcomes pets, no matter their size.
➕ E9 ✉ 171 W. Randolph Street ☎ 312/236-0123; 800/643-1500 🚇 Brown, Orange, Pink Lines: Washington/Wells; Blue, Brown and Green Lines: Clark/Lake 🚌 134, 135, 136, 156

HOTEL MONACO
monaco-chicago.com
Stylish striped wallpaper and offbeat colors provide zip to this 192-room boutique hotel in the Loop. Request a

room with a window seat to enjoy the view. Free WiFi and a complimentary wine reception nightly.

▪ F9 ✉ 225 N. Wabash Avenue ☎ 312/960-8500 🚇 Brown, Orange, Green Lines: State/Lake; Red Line: Lake 🚌 2, 6, 29, 134, 135, 136, 146, 148

HOTEL ZACHARY

marriott.com

Hotel Zachary features 173 guest rooms, including 20 suites, elegantly designed with artistic touches throughout. It is conveniently located across from Wrigley Field, and within walking distance of restaurants and shops.

▪ Off map ✉ 3630 N. Clark Street ☎ 773/302-2300 🚇 Red Line: Addison 🚌 22, 152

KINZIE HOTEL

kinziehotel.com

Near downtown and the Magnificent Mile, this Italian-style boutique hotel serves a complimentary breakfast and nightly hors d'oeuvres.

▪ E9 ✉ 20 W. Kinzie Street ☎ 312/395-9000 🚇 Red Line: Grand 🚌 22, 36

MILLENNIUM KNICKERBOCKER

millenniumhotels.com

First built in 1927, its Martini Bar and Crystal Ballroom retain a feel for that era, although its 305 rooms are 21st-century standard.

▪ F6 ✉ 163 E. Walton Place ☎ 312/751-8100 🚇 Red Line: Chicago 🚌 143, 146, 147, 148, 151

RENAISSANCE CHICAGO

marriott.com

A great Loop location, 520 spacious rooms and 40 suites make this hotel a good choice. Facilities include an indoor pool and a fitness center.

▪ E9 ✉ 1 W. Wacker Drive ☎ 866/238-4218 🚇 Red Line: Lake; Brown, Orange, Green: State/Lake 🚌 2, 6, 29, 36, 62, 146, 148

ST. JANE HOTEL

stjanehotel.com

Located in an iconic 1920s art deco skyscraper, this hotel is an 8-minute walk to Millennium Park.

▪ F9 ✉ 230 N. Michigan Avenue ☎ 312/345-1000 🚇 Red Line: Lake; Brown, Orange, Green Lines: State/Lake 🚌 3, 4, 6, 20, 26, 66, 124, 143, 146, 147, 148, 151, 157

SOFITEL CHICAGO WATER TOWER

sofitel-chicago.com

This striking glass hotel from French hoteliers Sofitel has views of 875 N. Michigan Avenue and a smart Mag Mile locale. There are comfortable and modern furnishings in the rooms.

▪ F7 ✉ 20 E. Chestnut Street ☎ 312/324-4000 🚇 Red Line: Chicago 🚌 36, 66

THE WHITEHALL

thewhitehallhotel.com

First opened in the 1920s, this 222-room hotel now has English-style furniture and modern amenities.

▪ F7 ✉ 105 E. Delaware Place ☎ 312/944-6300; 800/948-4255 🚇 Red Line: Chicago 🚌 36, 66, 143, 146, 147, 148, 151

THE PLACE TO BE SEEN

Two W Hotels make seeing and being seen as much a part of the stay as a night's rest. The W Hotel Lakeshore (✉ 644 N. Lake Shore Drive ☎ 312/943-9200) harbors the intimate The Living Room Bar on an upper floor with skyline views and the W Hotel City Center (✉ 172 W. Adams Street ☎ 312/332-1200) in the Loop draws the after-work crowd where mixologists craft elegant cocktails (whotels.com).

Luxury Hotels

CHICAGO ATHLETIC ASSOCIATION HOTEL

chicagoathletichotel.com

Once a men's athletic club, this architecturally stunning building was meticulously restored and made into a hotel with a games room and indoor pool. The crown jewel is Cindy's, its rooftop restaurant and bar with killer views of Millennium Park.

➕ F10 ✉ 12 S. Michigan Avenue ☎ 312/792-3581 🚇 Brown, Orange, Purple, Pink, Green Lines: Washington/Wabash 🚌 3, 4, 6, 26, 143

THE DRAKE

thedrakehotel.com

The ornate Gold Coast Ballroom is evidence that The Drake was modeled on an Italian Renaissance palace. Take afternoon tea in Palm Court, which has been serving tea to guests for a century.

➕ F6 ✉ 140 E. Walton Place ☎ 312/787-2200 🚇 Red Line: Chicago 🚌 143, 146, 147, 148, 151

FAIRMONT HOTEL

fairmont.com/chicago

Winning views over Millennium Park, the city and the lake; the 692 rooms are comfortable and tasteful. The fitness center is open 24 hours.

➕ F9 ✉ 200 N. Columbus Drive ☎ 312/565-8000; 866/540-4408 🚇 Red Line: Lake 🚌 4, 6, 20, 60

FOUR SEASONS HOTEL CHICAGO

fourseasons.com/chicago

A whim-catering hotel popular with celebrities. The in-room ice-cream-sundae delivery is particularly popular.

➕ F7 ✉ 120 E. Delaware Place ☎ 312/280-8800 🚇 Red Line: Chicago 🚌 143, 146, 147, 148, 151

THE LANGHAM CHICAGO

langhamhotels.com

Ranked as one of the best hotels in the US, The Langham sits along a riverfront spot in the city's center. Expect good service and spacious, modern rooms and an indoor pool. The restaurant, Travelle Kitchen + Bar, is among the best in the city.

➕ F9 ✉ 330 N. Wabash Avenue ☎ 312/923-9988 🚇 Brown, Green, Pink, Purple Lines: State/Lake; Blue Line: Clark/Lake; Red Line: Grand 🚌 29

PARK HYATT CHICAGO

parkchicago.hyatt.com

The best rooms, and the hotel's highly regarded NoMI restaurant, peer directly over the Historic Water Tower. Fine art complements the modern interiors.

➕ F7 ✉ 800 N. Michigan Avenue ☎ 312/335-1234 🚇 Red Line: Chicago 🚌 66, 125, 143, 146, 147, 148, 151

THE PENINSULA CHICAGO

peninsula.com

A gilded link in the Asia-based chain, the Peninsula Chicago has a lap pool with skyline views, a spa, luxurious rooms and exemplary service to match.

➕ F7 ✉ 108 E. Superior Street ☎ 312/337-2888 🚇 Red Line: Chicago 🚌 143, 146, 147, 148, 151

ROOFTOP BARS

Chicago's swankiest hotels have gorgeous rooftop bars. Chicago Athletic Association Hotel, LondonHouse Hotel and theWit are among the busiest, the most scenic—and the priciest.

Use this section to familiarize yourself with travel to and within Chicago. Planning can help save money: Consider a multi-day Ventra Card visitor's pass that allows unlimited trips on the mass transit system.

Planning Ahead

When To Go

June, July and August are the busiest months, but the weather can be tryingly hot—May, September and October months have warm but less extreme weather. Events and festivals take place year-round, however, major conventions in May, September, October and November cause hotel space to be scarce.

AVERAGE DAILY MAXIMUM TEMPERATURES

JAN	FEB	MAR	APR	MAY	JUN	JUL	AUG	SEP	OCT	NOV	DEC
22°F	26°F	37°F	49°F	59°F	69°F	74°F	72°F	65°F	53°F	40°F	27°F
-6°C	-3°C	3°C	9°C	15°C	21°C	23°C	22°C	18°C	12°C	4°C	-3°C

Spring (mid-March to May) Very changeable; sometimes snow, sometimes sun, but generally mild.

Summer (June to mid-September) Varies from warm to very hot, sometimes uncomfortably so, with high humidity.

Fall (mid-September to October) Though changeable, it is often mild with sunny days.

Winter (November to mid-March) Often very cold with heavy snow and strong winds. Winds can be strong any time and particularly cold when, usually in winter, they come from the north.

WHAT'S ON

January/February *Chinese New Year*: In Chinatown.

March *St. Patrick's Day*: Celebrations and a parade.

March/April *Baseball season opens.*

May *Polish Constitution Day* (first Sat): Polish cultural events and a parade.

Chicago Antiques + Art + Design Show at theMart.

June *Chicago Blues Festival*: Local and international artists perform in Millennium Park.

Printers Row Lit Fest: Used-book shops host events.

Chicago Gospel Festival: Gospel music in Millennium Park.

Mid-June to Labor Day *Ravinia Festival*: Chicago Symphony Orchestra, pop, folk and rock music, with picnicking on the lawns.

July *Taste of Chicago*: Five-day feeding frenzy, thousands sample dishes from city restaurants.

Independence Day (Jul 4): Special events include fireworks at Navy Pier.

August *Chicago Air & Water Show*: Spectacular stunts performed along the lakefront.

September *Chicago Jazz Festival*: Free jazz concerts in Millennium Park.

October *Chicago Marathon. Open House Chicago:* Free entry to hundreds of buildings, opened by Chicago Architecture Center.

November/December *Festival of Lights:* Lights along the Magnificent Mile.

Wright Plus Housewalk: Visit Oak Park homes designed by Frank Lloyd Wright.

Chicago Online

cityofchicago.org
The city government website. Chicagoans use this to pay their bills but it also includes plenty of interest to visitors.

choosechicago.com
Geared toward visitors to Chicago, and features neighborhood highlights and happenings throughout the city.

enjoyillinois.org
Official site of the Illinois Office of Tourism.

chicagotribune.com
The online version of Chicago's biggest-circulation daily newspaper.

Chicago.Eater.com
An reliable website packed with restaurant reviews and news about Chicago's restaurants.

chicagoreader.com
The website of the city's long-established alternative weekly newspaper, the *Chicago Reader*, with a different slant on city affairs and its own recommendations for entertainment.

chicagotribune.com/redeye
The online version of its daily print issue, RedEye Chicago shares the best things to eat, drink or do in Chicago, with up-to-date events.

chicago.metromix.com
Chicago edition of a national site providing informative listings, covering events, museums, dining, nightlife and more.

CTABusTracker.com
Helps you find out how far away your bus is—especially valuable when the weather's bad.

DivvyBikes.com
Chicago's bikeshare system is an alternative and sometimes faster way to get around town.

USEFUL WEBSITES

fodors.com
A complete travel-planning site. Research prices and the weather; reserve air tickets, cars and rooms; ask questions (and get answers) from fellow visitors; and find links to other sites.

transitchicago.com
The website of the Chicago Transit Authority explains all there is to know about using the city's buses and El trains, the fares and ticket types, with route maps that can be downloaded and lots more.

Getting There

ENTRY REQUIREMENTS

Visitors to Chicago from outside the US require a machine-readable passport, valid for at least six months. Passports issued on or after October 26, 2004 must include a biometric identifier; UK passports already issued will still qualify for up to 90 days visa-free travel in the visa-waiver scheme. Visitors using the visa-waiver program must register their details online before traveling. Check the current situation and requirements before you leave home (US Embassy visa and ESTA information: usembassy.gov; British Embassy in the US: britainusa.com).
Be sure to leave plenty of time to clear security as the levels of checks are constantly being stepped up.

AIRPORTS

Chicago's O'Hare International Airport is 17 miles (27km) northwest of the Loop and takes all international flights and most domestic flights. Midway Airport, 8 miles (13km) southwest of the Loop, is primarily a domestic hub but also handles international travel.

FROM O'HARE INTERNATIONAL AIRPORT

For information on O'Hare International Airport, call 773/686-3700 or visit ohare.com. GO Airport Express (tel 888/284-3826, airportexpress.com) runs minibuses between O'Hare and the Loop every 10–15 minutes 6am–11.30pm (fare $32; journey time 60 minutes). Pick them up from outside the arrivals terminal. Make a reservation for the trip from your hotel to the airport.

Chicago Transit Authority (tel 888/968-7282, transitchicago.com) operates Blue Line trains between O'Hare and the Loop (24 hours; journey time 45 minutes; fare $5). Follow the signs from the arrivals hall to the station. However, it is safer to take a taxi late at night from either airport. Taxis wait outside the arrivals terminal and the fare to the Loop or nearby hotels is about $35–$40.

ARRIVING AT MIDWAY AIRPORT

For information about Midway Airport, call 773/838-0600 or visit flychicago.com/midway. GO Airport Express runs minibuses to the Loop every 15 minutes 6am–10.30pm (fare around

$28–$30; journey time 60 minutes). Pick the minibus up from outside Door 3, located on the lower level near Baggage Claim.

Chicago Transit Authority runs Orange Line trains to the Loop from 4 or 4.30am–1am (fare $2.50; journey time 30 minutes). Taxis wait at the arrivals terminal. The fare to the Loop or nearby hotels is approximately $35–$40.

ARRIVING BY BUS
Greyhound buses (tel 800/231-2222, 312/408-5821, greyhound.com) arrive at 630 W. Harrison Street, six blocks southwest of the Loop. MegaBus (tel 877-462/6342, 773/890-6300, megabus.com), which serves eight Midwestern states with budget-priced fares, stops at W. Polk Street between S. Clinton Street and S. Canal Street.

ARRIVING BY CAR
Chicago has good Interstate access: I-80 and I-90 are the major east–west routes; I-55 and I-57 arrive from the south. I-94 runs through the city linking the north and south suburbs. To reach the Loop from O'Hare Airport use I-90. From Midway Airport take I-55, linking with the northbound I-90/94 for the Loop. Journeys take from 45 to 90 minutes and 30 to 60 minutes respectively depending on traffic and weather. Try to avoid rush hours, 7–9am and 4–7pm.

There are more than half-dozen auto rental agencies at both O'Hare International Airport and Midway Airport. Rates usually start in the range of $70 to $100 per day, $150 to $200 per week, with fuel as an extra charge. Check agencies for local specials.

ARRIVING BY TRAIN
Amtrak trains (tel 800/872-7245, amtrak.com) use Chicago's Union Station, at the junction of W. Adams and S. Canal streets. Amtrak can also be a great option for visitors traveling beyond Chicago. Trains serve the entire country.

CHICAGO GREETERS

Choose Chicago, the official destination marketing organization for the city, runs a program to match volunteer residents with inquiring visitors. Chicago Greeters (chicagogreeter.com) won't meet you at the airport, nor even on the day that you arrive, but by prior arrangement will spend two to four hours showing you around the city and providing an insider's point of view. The service is free but requires a seven-day advance registration via the website chicagogreeter.com. Greeters will escort one to six visitors on the itinerary of their choice, ranging from outings themed on food or history to itineraries that look at a specific neighborhood.

Getting Around

DRIVING IN CHICAGO

Driving in the city is stressful: Use public transportation. Many hotels have parking lots, otherwise overnight parking is difficult and very costly. During the day, street parking is often limited to two hours; spaces in the Loop are near impossible to find.

VISITORS WITH DISABILITIES

Legislation aimed at improving access for visitors with disabilities in Chicago means that all recently built structures have to provide disabled access; the newer they are, the stricter the rules. Many older buildings, including most hotels, have been converted to ensure they comply. Both airports are accessible, as are many CTA buses and El stations. For details log on to transitchicago.com or cityofchicago.org/disabilities.

Much of Chicago can be explored on foot. To travel between neighborhoods use the network of buses and El (elevated) trains, which travel above and below ground. Many El trains operate 24-hours a day. Best value to use for many journeys are the Visitor Pass tickets valid for 1–7 days (see below). Buy them from the airport, CTA stations, from major museums and the Visitor Information center (for information call 888/968-7282 or visit transitchicago.com/travel_information). Cash and multi-use plastic cards can be used. Taxis wait outside hotels, conference halls and major El stations, or can be hailed. Uber and Lyft ride services are easily available, using their companies' apps.

- If traveling outside the Loop at night, it is best to take a taxi rather than public transportation.
- Metra commuter trains are best for visiting some areas (metrarail.com).
- For information on the El and buses contact Chicago Transit Authority on 888/968-7282 or Metra on 312/322-6900 or 312/322-6777.

THE EL

- Fare: $2.50 Ventra Card, plus 25¢ transfer. Transfer to a different line (or to a bus) within two hours: 25¢ (free within Loop). A second transfer within the same two hours is free. Children 7–11 ride for $1.25 with card, plus 15¢ transfer. Kids under age 7 travel free with a fee-paying customer.
- Plastic transit cards are the only way to pay fares. Cards are dispensed for cash, credit-card or debit-card payments from automated machines. Replenish existing cards here too.
- Visitor passes valid for 1 day ($10), 3 days ($20), 7 days ($28) or 30 days ($105) permit unlimited rides on buses and trains. The pass activates the first time you use it and is good for the consecutive number of calendar days shown on the front of the pass. You can order them before you arrive at the CTA website (transitchicago.com) or buy them at many hotels, Chicago visitor centers and O'Hare and Midway CTA stations.

- All stations have automatic ticket machines.
- Eight color-coded lines run through the city and converge on the Loop.
- On weekdays 6am–7pm, some trains stop only at alternate stations, plus all major stations. Station announcements will alert you to the change.
- Many trains run 24 hours; frequency is reduced on weekends and during the night. Several lines suspend service between roughly 1am and 5am.
- Some stations are closed on weekends.

BUSES
- Fare: $2.50 with a transit card or cash (no change given). Transfer to a different route (or to the El) within two hours: 25¢.
- Plastic transit cards are the simplest way to pay fares (and the only option for the El). They are sold at all CTA train stations and Visitor Information centers.

SCHEDULE AND MAP INFORMATION
- CTA maps showing El and bus routes are available from El station fare booths.
- Bus routes are shown at stops.
- The CTA website (transitchicago.com) contains all transportation schedules and maps and offers directions and information on the best way to get to the city's most popular tourist attractions.

TAXIS
- Fares are generally $3.25 for the first mile and $2.25 for each additional mile. The second additional passenger costs $1 and each further additional passenger costs 50¢. There is an airport departure tax payable of $4.
- Hotel, restaurant and nightclub staff will order a taxi on request or you can phone: Checker (tel 312/243-2537), Flash (tel 773/561-4444 or Yellow (tel 312/829-4222 or text 312/520-3096).
- To request a wheelchair-accessible taxi cab, call 855/928-1010 or visit opentaxis.com.

GOING BY WATER

In spring and summer the Chicago Water Taxi (☎ 312/337-1446; chicagowatertaxi.com) offers a ferry service from 6.30am to sundown. There are seven stops along the Chicago River: Madison Street, LaSalle Street, Michigan Avenue, Clark Street/Riverwalk, North Avenue/Sheffield, Chicago Avenue and Chinatown. One-way fares cost $6; a day pass costs $10.

MAPPING CHICAGO

Most of Chicago is laid out on a grid system with ground zero at State, which runs north–south, and Madison, east–west, in the Loop. Each block number changes by 100, with eight blocks equaling roughly one mile (1.6km). For instance, 800 N. State Street means the location is eight blocks north of the baseline intersection, while 110 E. Madison lies on the second block east of it. Even-number addresses belong to the north or west side of a street; odd numbers mean the location is on the south or east side of a street.

Essential Facts

Travel insurance is essential for the US because of the high cost of any kind of medical treatment. Check your insurance policy and buy a supplementary policy if needed. A minimum of $1 million medical cover is recommended. Choose a policy that also includes trip cancelation, baggage loss and document loss.

MONEY

Dollar bills (notes) come in denominations of $1, $5, $10, $20, $50 and $100; coins are 25¢ (a quarter), 10¢ (a dime), 5¢ (a nickel) and 1¢ (a penny).

CUSTOMS REGULATIONS

● Duty-free allowances include 1 liter of alcoholic spirits or wine (no one under 21 may bring alcohol into the US), 200 cigarettes or 100 cigars, and up to $800-worth of gifts.
● Some medication bought over the counter abroad may be prescription-only in the US and may be confiscated. Bring a doctor's certificate for essential medication.
● It is forbidden to bring food, seeds and plants into the US.

ELECTRICITY

● The electricity supply is 110 volts; 60 cycles AC current.
● US appliances use two-prong plugs. European appliances require an adaptor.

ETIQUETTE

● Smoking is banned in all public buildings, restaurants, bars and on public transportation.
● Tipping is voluntary, but the following are usually expected: 15–20 percent for taxis and restaurants; $1 per bag for a hotel porter.

MEDICAL TREATMENT

● For doctors, ask hotel staff or the Chicago Medical Society (tel 312/670-2550).
● In an emergency go to a hospital with a 24-hour emergency room, such as Northwestern Memorial Hospital at 251 E. Huron Street (tel 312/926-2000).
● If in need of dental care, the Chicago Dental Society (tel 312/836-7300) will refer you to a dentist in your area.
● There are also Minute Clinic or Immediate Care Clinic outlets throughout the city, primarily at Walgreens and CVS locations.

MEDICINES

● Visit a Walgreens or CVS for pharmacy needs. Visitors from Europe will find many familiar medicines under unfamiliar names. Some drugs available over the counter at home are prescription only in the US.

- If you use medication, bring a supply (but note the warning in Customs Regulations, ▷ 120). If you intend to buy prescription drugs in the US, bring a note from your doctor.
- There are many late-night and 24-hour pharmacies around the city, including CVS Pharmacy within Target (401 E. Illinois Street, tel 312/894-1764, and several branches of Walgreens (757 N. Michigan Avenue, tel 312/664-8686; 30 N. Michigan Avenue, tel 312/332-3540; and 641 N. Clark Street, tel 312/587-1416).

MONEY MATTERS
- Most banks have ATMs, which accept credit cards registered in other countries that are linked to the Cirrus or Plus networks. Ensure your personal identification number is valid in the US: four- and six-figure numbers are usual.
- Credit cards are widely accepted.
- US dollar traveler's checks function like cash in most shops; $20 and $50 denominations are most useful. Seeking to exchange these (or foreign currency) at a bank can be difficult and commissions can be high.
- A 10.25 percent sales tax is added to marked retail prices, except on groceries and prescription drugs.
- A Chicago CityPASS or a Go Chicago Card offer multiple discounts to major tourist destinations (go to smartdestinations.com or citypass.com/chicago).

NEWSPAPERS AND MAGAZINES
- Major daily newspapers are the *Chicago Tribune* and the *Chicago Sun-Times* (international, national and local stories).
- A good free weekly is the *Chicago Reader*.
- Glossy monthly magazines such as the *Chicago* reflect the interests of well-heeled Chicagoans. The *Windy City Times* highlights news of interest to the LGBTQ+ community.
- Free magazines, such as *Where Chicago*, are aimed at tourists and can often be found in hotel lobbies.

TOURIST OFFICES
The visitor information centers are in the lower level of the Macy's building (✉ 111 N. State Street ☎ 888/330-5008), at Millennium Park Welcome Center (✉ 201 E. Randolph Street), Navy Pier Guest Services (✉ 600 E. Grand Avenue), or visit ChooseChicago.com.

NATIONAL HOLIDAYS
- New Year's Day (Jan 1)
- Martin Luther King Day (third Mon in Jan)
- President's Day (third Mon in Feb)
- Memorial Day (last Mon in May)
- Independence Day (Jul 4)
- Labor Day (first Mon in Sep)
- Columbus Day (second Mon in Oct)
- Veterans Day (Nov 11)
- Thanksgiving Day (fourth Thu in Nov)
- Christmas Day (Dec 25)

EMERGENCY PHONE NUMBERS
- Fire, police or ambulance ☎ 911 (no money required)
- Rape Crisis Hotline ☎ 888/293-2080

LOST AND FOUND

- O'Hare International Airport ☎ 800/832-6352
- The El and buses: Chicago Transit Authority ☎ 888/968-7282; Metra ☎ 312/322-7819

OPENING HOURS

- Stores: Mon–Sat from 9 or 10 until 6 or 7. Most stores are also open Sun noon–6. Department stores and malls keep longer hours. Other stores, such as bookshops, may open in the evenings.
- Banks: Mon–Fri 9–5, with some branches open later once a week.
- Post offices: the downtown location, at 211 S. Clark Street, is open Mon–Fri 7am–6pm; Harrison Street location is open Mon–Fri 8.30–noon, Sat 9am–11pm, Sun 10am–9pm.

POST OFFICES

- Minimum charge for sending a postcard anywhere outside the US is $1.15.
- To find the nearest post office, ask at your hotel. Most open Mon–Fri 8.30–5, Sat 9–2 (varies by location).

SENSIBLE PRECAUTIONS

- By day, the Loop and major areas of interest to visitors are relatively safe. Some tourist sights involve journeys through unwelcoming areas; so consider discussing your itinerary with hotel staff and heed their advice.
- After dark, stay in established nightlife areas. River North and River West, Rush and Division streets, and Lakeview/Wrigleyville are fairly safe if you use common-sense precautions. If you're alone, wait for a cab inside a club or restaurant, or where staff can see you.
- Neighborhoods can change character within a few blocks. Stick to safe, busy and well-lit streets.
- Carry shoulder bags strapped across your chest. Keep belongings within sight and reach.
- Store valuables in your hotel's safe and never carry more money than you need.
- Replacing a stolen passport begins with a visit or phone call to your nearest consular office.
- Report any stolen item to the nearest police precinct. It is unlikely that stolen goods will be recovered, but the police will fill in the forms your insurance company needs.

STUDENT VISITORS
● An International Student Identity Card (ISIC) reduces admission prices to many attractions.
● Anyone aged under 21 is forbidden to buy or drink alcohol and may be denied admission to some nightclubs.

TELEPHONES
● Calls from hotel rooms are usually more expensive than those from a cell phone.
● Many businesses have toll-free numbers, prefixed with 800, 866 or 888.
● Most US phones use touch-tone dialing, enabling callers to access extensions directly.
● To call Chicago from the UK dial 001 followed by the full number. To call the UK from Chicago dial 011 44 and omit the first zero from the area code.

TOILETS
● Most department stores, malls and hotel lobbies have adequate toilets.

TV AND RADIO
Chicago's main TV channels are 2 WBBM (CBS); 5 WMAQ (NBC); 7 WLS (ABC); 9 WGN (local WB affiliate); 11 WTTW (PBS); 32 WFLD (Fox).
Radio stations include:
● Classical: WFMT 98.7FM
● Country: WUSN 99.5FM
● National Public Radio: WBEZ 91.5FM
● News: WBBM 780AM
● R&B: WGCI 107.5FM
● Talk radio and local sports: WGN 720AM; WSCR 670AM; WLS 890AM; ESPN CHICAGO AM1000

TRAVELING WITH CHILDREN

Chicago is a destination that welcomes children. Classic sights like the Willis Tower Observatory, Navy Pier, Shedd Aquarium, Field Museum, Museum of Science and Industry and the Chicago Children's Museum delight all ages, but especially kids. Furthermore, adults don't have to sacrifice their own interests to those of a child. The Art Institute of Chicago runs an excellent visitor's program for children; check their website (artic.edu) for a month-by-month guide to the activities. The Crown Fountain in Millennium Park is a popular spot for kids to play in summer in the water. When rest is required for little legs, go passive sightseeing by riding the El or taking a water taxi.

CONSULATES		
Germany	✉ 676 N. Michigan Avenue, Suite 3200	☎ 312/202-0480
Ireland	✉ 1 E. Wacker Drive, Suite 1820	☎ 312/337-1868
Portugal	✉ Aon Center, 200 E. Randolph Street, Suite 2200	☎ 312/345-1149
Spain	✉ 180 N. Michigan Avenue, # 1500	☎ 312/782-4588
UK	✉ 625 N. Michigan Avenue, Suite 2200	☎ 312/970-3800

Timeline

WINDY CITY

In 1893, Chicago hosted the World's Columbian Exposition. The hyperbole of politicians caused one journalist to describe Chicago as "the windy city," an enduring epithet.

THE HAYMARKET RIOT

Heavy-handed police tactics in a series of labor disputes prompted a group of German-born anarchists to organize a protest rally on May 4, 1886, in Haymarket Square. A bomb thrown from the crowd exploded among the police lines; the explosion and the police use of firearms killed seven people and wounded 150. Seven anarchists received death sentences. In 1893, a full pardon was granted to three imprisoned anarchists, due to the lack of evidence linking any of the anarchists to the bomb.

1673 Missionary Jacques Marquette and explorer Louis Joliet discover the 1.5-mile (2.4-km) American Indian portage trail linking the Mississippi River and the Great Lakes—the site of future Chicago.

1779–81 Trapper and trader Jean Baptiste Point du Sable, a Haitian, becomes Chicago's first settler.

1812 Fort Dearborn, one of several forts protecting trade routes, is attacked by American Indians.

1830 Chicago is selected as the site of a canal linking the Great Lakes and the Mississippi.

1870 Chicago's population reaches 330,000 from 30,000 in 1850. Many arrivals are Irish, who find work building the railways.

1871 The Great Chicago Fire kills 300 people.

1894 A strike at the Pullman rail company unites black and white workers for the first time.

1906 Upton Sinclair's novel, *The Jungle,* focuses national attention on the conditions endured by workers in the notorious Union Stockyards.

1908 Chicago Cubs win baseball's World Series for a second successive year.

1914 With World War I, Chicago's black population increases as African Americans from the Deep South move north to work industrial jobs.

1919–33 Prohibition. Chicago's transport links make it a natural place for alcohol manufacture and distribution. Armed crime mobs thrive.

1950s In South Side clubs, rhythmic and electrified Chicago blues evolves.

1955 Richard J. Daley is elected mayor and dominates Chicago political life for 21 years.

1968 Police attack anti-Vietnam War protesters in Grant Park during the Democratic National Convention.

1974 Completion of Sears Tower (now Willis Tower), the world's tallest building until 1996.

1992 A collapsing wall causes the Chicago River to flood the Loop.

2009 Illinois senator and Chicago resident Barack Obama is sworn in as the 44th President of the United States.

2011 Richard M. Daley, Chicago's longest-serving mayor (22 years), leaves office and Rahm Emanuel becomes the 55th Mayor of Chicago.

2016 The Chicago Cubs baseball team wins the World Series for the first time in 108 years.

GANGSTERS

Intended to encourage sobriety and family life, Prohibition (1919–33) provided a great stimulus to organized crime. The exploits of Chicago-based gangsters such as Al Capone became legendary. Though depicted frequently on films and TV, shoot-outs between rival gangs were rare. An exception was the 1929 Valentine's Day Massacre, when Capone's gang eliminated their archrivals in a hail of machine-gun fire. Wealthy enough to bribe corruptible politicians and police, the gangsters seemed invincible, but the gangster era—though not necessarily the gangs—ended with Capone's imprisonment in 1931 and the repeal of Prohibition.

From left to right: Directions to Clarke House; a baseball game in progress at Wrigley Field; an old copy of the Chicago Daily Tribune; *the Hyatt Center soars skyward*

Index

Chicago 25 Best

WRITTEN BY Mick Sinclair and Elaine Glusac
UPDATED BY Megy Karydes
SERIES EDITOR Clare Ashton
COVER DESIGN Jessica Gonzalez
DESIGN WORK Liz Baldin
IMAGE RETOUCHING AND REPRO Ian Little

ISBN 978-1-64097-339-8

TENTH EDITION

Printed and bound in China by 1010 Printing Group Limited.

10 9 8 7 6 5 4 3 2 1

A05743
Maps in this title produced from mapping © MAIRDUMONT / Falk Verlag 2017, map data © Global Mapping (globalmapping.uk.com) and data available from openstreetmap.org © under the Open Database License found at opendatacommons.org
Transport maps © Communicarta Ltd, UK

We would like to thank the following photographers, companies and picture libraries for their assistance in the preparation of this book:

All images are copyright AA/C Sawyer except:

2–3, 4t Choose Chicago; 5t Choose Chicago; 5b Choose Chicago/© City of Chicago; 6t Choose Chicago; 6cr AA/P Wood; 6br Choose Chicago/Adam Alexander Photography; 7t Choose Chicago; 7cl Choose Chicago/© City of Chicago; 7cr Choose Chicago/© City of Chicago; 7bl Choose Chicago/Clayton Hauck; 7bc Choose Chicago/Clayton Hauck; 7br 360Chicago; 8–9 Choose Chicago; 10t Choose Chicago; 10c Choose Chicago/Adam Alexander Photography; 10/11 Choose Chicago/Adam Alexander Photography; 11t Choose Chicago; 11ct Choose Chicago/Adam Alexander Photography; 11cb Choose Chicago/ Adam Alexander Photography; 12t Choose Chicago; 12b Choose Chicago/ Adam Alexander Photography; 13t Choose Chicago; 13c Choose Chicago/© City of Chicago; 13cb–14t Choose Chicago; 14ct Choose Chicago/Adam Alexander Photography; 14c–14cb Choose Chicago/Clayton Hauck; 14b Choose Chicago/ Adam Alexander Photography; 15, 16t Choose Chicago; 16ct Ian G Dagnall/ Alamy Stock Photo; 16b The Alley Stores; 16/7c Ian Dagnall/Alamy Stock Photo; 17t Choose Chicago; 17ct Chicago Athletic Association Hotel; 17cb Digital Vision; 17b Chicago Cubs; 18t Choose Chicago; 18c Choose Chicago/© City of Chicago; 18cb Jason Lindsey/Alamy Stock Photo; 18b Peninsula Chicago; 20 The Ledge at Willis Tower; 24r Chicago Architecture Foundation; 28t Skydeck Chicago at Willis Tower(2); 28bl Bloomberg/Getty Images; 28br–29 Skydeck Chicago at Willis Tower (3); 30t, 30br, 31t AA/P Wood; 31bl Felix Lipov/Alamy Stock Photo; 31br AA/P Wood; 32 AA/P Wood; 33–34 Macy's; 35, 36 Digital Vision; 42l, 43t, 42/43c , 43cr Adler Planetarium; 44tl, 44cl, 44/45 Courtesy of Art Institute of Chicago; 46t, 47t, 47cl, 47cr © Field Museum; 48t, 48cl Courtesy of Shedd Aquarium; 48cr Courtesy of Shedd Aquarium; 49 Shedd Aquarium/Brenna Hernandez; 51t AA/P Wood; 51bl Choose Chicago/© City of Chicago; 52 AA/P Wood; 53t AA/ Slidefile; 54 Imagestate; 55 Choose Chicago/© City of Chicago; 58tl 360Chicago; 58cl 360Chicago; 59t 360Chicago; 60 photos of Carl Hammer Gallery, Inc./by Carl Hammer; 61 Courtesy of Weinberg/Newton Gallery_Kyle Flubacker; 62t Lincoln Park Zoo; 62cr Lincoln Park Zoo; 63cl Lincoln Park Zoo; 63cr Lincoln Park Zoo; 64 Navy Pier; 65t Navy Pier; 65c Navy Pier; 66l Choose Chicago/© City of Chicago; 66r Choose Chicago/Adam Alexander Photography; 68l Choose Chicago; 69t AA/P Wood; 69b Courtesy of Chicago Children's Museum; 70t AA/P Wood; 70bl Courtesy of International Museum of Surgical Sciences; 70br Choose Chicago/© City of Chicago; 71t AA/P Wood; 71b Choose Chicago/© City of Chicago; 72t AA/P Wood; 72br AA/P Wood; 73 AA/P Wood; 74 AA/S McBride; 75 AA/S McBride; 76 Digital Vision; 77 Digital Vision; 78t Digital Vision; 81 imageBROKER/Alamy Stock Photo; 84 Choose Chicago/© City of Chicago; 85l DuSable Museum of African American History; 85r DuSable Museum of African American History; 87r Courtesy of Glessner House; 88l © Courtesy of Museum of Science and Industry; 89tr © Courtesy of Museum of Science and Industry; 89cr © Courtesy of Museum of Science and Industry; 90t AA/P Wood; 91t AA/P Wood; 91b Courtesy of Frank Lloyd Wright Trust. Photographer: Tim Long; 92 AA/P Wood; 95 Choose Chicago/© City of Chicago; 99l Neighborly Store, Chicago; 99r Neighborly Store, Chicago; 100l Courtesy of Frank Lloyd Wright House; 101l Choose Chicago/© City of Chicago; 101r Chicago Cubs; 102t AA/P Wood; 102bl AA/P Wood; 103 The Alley Stores; 104 Digital Vision; 105 Choose Chicago/Adam Alexander Photography; 106 Choose Chicago/Adam Alexander Photography; 108c Choose Chicago/Adam Alexander Photography; 108cb AA/S McBride; 108b Stockbyte; 124bl AA/P Wood; 125bl AA/P Wood; 125br Choose Chicago/© City of Chicago.

Every effort has been made to trace the copyright holders, and we apologise in advance for any accidental errors. We would be happy to apply the corrections in the following edition of this publication.

Titles in the Series